RECOLLECTIONS OF
SEVENTY YEARS

F. B. Sanborn

The Gale Library of Lives and Letters
American Writers Series

RECOLLECTIONS
OF SEVENTY YEARS
By F. B. SANBORN
OF CONCORD

IN TWO VOLUMES

VOLUME ONE

ARTI et VERITATI

BOSTON
RICHARD G. BADGER
THE GORHAM PRESS
1909

REPUBLISHED BY GALE RESEARCH COMPANY, BOOK TOWER, DETROIT, 1967

CONTENTS

VOLUME I

ILLUSTRATIONS

VOLUME I

PREFACE

THIS may be termed a book of Old Age; and few themes have been more written about. But seldom have the young taken it for their theme, nor can a very young person know what age actually is. I remember, when a boy of eleven, looking at my father when he was approaching forty, and wondering if I should ever be so old as he then seemed. Well, here I am, nearly twice that age—and yet not feeling in myself that inactive and morose condition so often associated with advanced years. Shakespeare's old Mortimer on his deathbed typifies another spirit in age—saying to his nephew, the ambitious York—

> But now thy uncle is removing hence,
> As princes do their seats, when they are cloyed
> With long continuance in a settled place.

Such lordly condescension toward this mundane life is not to be generally expected—perhaps should not be encouraged in Christians—but it has its advantages. The love of life is natural, and probably stronger in the old than the young, judging by my own experience, who at seventeen was more ready to leave this world than at seventy-five. Yet one must not cling to earthly life too closely. Emerson opened his essay on Old Age with an allusion to President Quincy's speech at the Phi Beta din-

ner of 1861, when in his ninetieth year. I missed
that, but heard his shorter speech the day before at
the Commencement dinner in Harvard Hall. The
hale old man made a jest, and in so doing illus-
trated that strange fact, of inheritance from a single ancestor out of the thousands from whom each
one of us is descended. Shortly before, at the
Hasty Pudding Club I had seen a young Quincy,
his grandson, acting in a comedy (as I had done
seven years before, in the same place), and he
twisted his expressive face exactly as the grand-
sire did afterwards in his joke at the Commencement dinner.

We inherit our capacity for age, as we do our
stature and complexions; and we must use well
what was bequeathed, or we may curse the heri-
tage. Life is a loan, not a chattel, as Lucretius so
well said—

Vitaque mancipio nulli datur, omnibus usu.

We must pay for its use, and if we waste it must
make it good or give it up. Whether this new and
furious practice of athletics prolongs life I doubt;
it makes the young stronger, more agile, more ex-
pert; but is as likely to hasten death as to defer it.
Yet there is a view of long life worth mentioning,
as that of a very wise and heroic person, John
Brown of Osawatomie, of whom I have much to
tell in the pages of this book. Writing from his
Virginia prison, under sentence of death, forty-
nine years ago, he said:

" I have enjoyed much of life, and have been remarkably prosperous, having early learned to regard the welfare and prosperity of others as my own. I have never required a great amount of sleep; so that I conclude that I have already, though not quite 60, enjoyed full an average of working hours with those who reach their threescore years and ten. I have enjoyed life much; why should I complain on leaving it? I firmly believe that God reigns, and that he overrules all things in the best possible manner."

My view of life is quite that of my good old friend, the convict of Virginia. There is no better preparation for old age than such opinions; and my own experience has confirmed them. It was this tendency in myself which admitted me easily to the Concord circle of writers, to which, spiritually, Brown belonged, in spite of his Old Testament theology, which wore thin, as life advanced. Variety in unity was the Concord spirit, exemplified in Alcott, in Emerson, and perhaps most strikingly in Thoreau. His love of wild Nature and the Indian mode of life was one side of that singular character. But there was quite another side; a gentle, poetic aspect, in which the bow and arrow were laid apart, the flute taken up, and the soul attuned to melody. In this mood he was Virgilian; the shepherds of Mantua and the reeds of the Mincio never appeared to me quite so probable as when I rambled with him in Walden Woods or Estabrook Farm, or swam the Assabet on our way to the hill Anursnac. To compose verses and enwreathe our Yankee life with pastoral garlands then seemed natural and easy, as in his epigram on 'Smoke.' Here was the spirit of the Walden years crystallized into a stanza; here was the *much in little,* which is the secret of Concord authorship. Mystical were other utterances of the man, like this:

> I hearing get who had but ears,
>   And sight, who had but eyes before;
> Moments I live, who lived but years,
>   And Truth discern, who knew but Learning's lore.

The neglect of fame in Concord was sometimes from pride, as in Hawthorne, or carelessness, as in Channing, or humility, as in Emerson; but usually it proceeded from a clear view of its unworthiness, when contrasted with the inner motive and reward of the mystic. More than any writers of their century, they threw themselves at the feet of that 'Love whose other name is Justice,' as Emerson said; and their serene confidence, occasionally passing into spiritual pride, was born of this devotion to an ideal service—not Pantheistic, though it used the phrases of Pantheism, and as far as possible from the modern heresy of the Agnostics. This is their chief title to a place in literary history; they came within the scope of the Apostle's prediction of what will never fail; but " whether there be prophecies, they shall fail; whether there be tongues, they shall cease; whether there be knowledge, it shall vanish away." In this decay of learning, this frustration of intellectual vanity, this displacement of one science by another—each boasting itself im-

perishable, and each perishing—the soul of man
must ever take sanctuary with that poet who cried—

I will not doubt the love untold
    Which not my worth nor want hath bought;
Which wooed me young, and wooes me old,
    And to this evening hath me brought.

In the twenty-four chapters of these volumes, only a
part of what I remember has even been touched on;
and I have given up the original intent to relate my
connection with public charity and Social Science,
which occupied me much for more than thirty years.
That story may be told hereafter, and other matters may be dealt with, but here chiefly I deal with
the events of my first forty years.

The portraits, views and fac-similes which I have
inserted, at the request of the publisher, are mostly
hitherto unpublished, or else so long since or so privately printed that they will be new to most who
see the book. Errors will be found in its pages, but
not of intention. I have had my share of controversy, but seldom in personal quarrels; usually in
behalf of others, for whom I sought to present the
case as they could not or would not; and I am never
so well pleased as when truthfully corrected, as I
often have been and expect to be.

F. B. S.

Concord, December 15, 1908.

POLITICAL LIFE

RECOLLECTIONS
OF SEVENTY YEARS

CHAPTER I

Preliminary

THIS day, July 6, 1908, I begin such Recollections of my life and my acquaintances as occur to me, and have not been published elsewhere; including, however, many things which I have printed publicly or privately during the past half century; in course of which I have recalled and written out particulars that may be useful to me in this volume. Many of these have appeared in my "History of New Hampshire," or in the *Granite Monthly,* a New Hampshire local magazine; in the *Springfield Republican,* to which I have contributed for more than fifty years; in the Boston *Commonwealth,* between 1862 and 1868, and of late years in the printed proceedings of the Massachusetts Historical Society. Having recently published there something more than 100 pages concerning the early history of Kansas, I may also draw from that source some facts of importance.

I am now well along in my seventy-eighth year, having been born (on the estate of my ancestors for six generations, at Hampton Falls, N. H., and in a dwelling house now 165 years old) on the 15th of December, 1831; the son of Aaron Sanborn, then Town Clerk of the small municipality, and

Lydia Leavitt, his wife—the fifth of their seven children, of whom the eldest died in infancy. I was the second son, my older brother, the late Dr. Charles Henry Sanborn, being ten years my senior, and my youngest brother, Joseph Leavitt Sanborn, who died at St. Louis, Mo., in 1872, being twelve years younger than myself. An intermediate brother, Lewis Thomas Sanborn, was born in October, 1834; and my two sisters, Sarah Elizabeth and Helen Maria, had been born, respectively, in 1823 and 1830. My name, which is peculiar in its arrangement (Franklin Benjamin, instead of the customary Benjamin Franklin), is due to a whim of my father, who, as Town Clerk, could enter me by any name he pleased. I was really named for my grandfather, Benjamin Sanborn, and his father of the same name, which he took from a worthy uncle, Deacon Benjamin, grandson of the first emigrant Sanborn, John by name, who was a grandson of the founder of Hampton, Rev. Stephen Bachiler, an Oxford scholar of Queen Elizabeth's reign. But my Grandmother Leavitt, when I went to see her in the fine house under the four elms on the Kensington road, in view of the lovely Kensington hills, used to put her gentle hand on my head and call me " her little Dr. Franklin," and so the great doctor's surname was given me for a middle name. But my father, foreseeing that I should be called "Frank," as I always have been, declared that his son should not be known by his middle name, and therefore registered me in the reverse order of the two names.

DR. SANBORN'S HOME, HAMPTON FALLS.   OLD HOMESTEAD

THE LEAVITT HOMESTEAD, HAMPTON FALLS

It is a serious thought that I am now several years older than my father, who died in 1866, at 73, and but a few months younger than my Grandfather Leavitt, the squire of his neighborhood, who died before he was 78, in 1852. But my Grandfather Sanborn lived to be 87, and my mother to be 83—so that I may still have several years of inherited longevity before me. It is from the mother's side that we four brothers and my younger sister take our physical inheritance, though not her extreme beauty. She was of fair complexion, good feminine stature, with blue eyes, thick jet-black hair, a brilliant color, and a most amiable expression. My father was brown-haired, with dark eyes and of tall and slender stature, though of stalwart strength; a daring horseman, and deft with his hands for almost any farming or mechanical labor. His mood was serious, and in his later years stoical, with a touch of the cynic; upright and charitable, but seldom gracious, except to the poor, and rather severe with his children, who grew up to hold opinions quite unlike his own. In this he was the reverse of his father, who was the type of a smiling English yeoman, full of good will and hospitality, and at peace with all the world. He died when I was sixteen, but I do not remember that I ever heard from him a harsh or offensive word. In my childhood I slept with him, and had much of his society at other times. One of my earliest recollections is of being put early into his great bed, by which my beautiful mother sat and sung to me in her sweet voice, to a Hebrew air—

Hush, my dear—lie still and slumber!
Holy angels guard thy bed;
Heavenly blessings without number
Gently falling on thy head.

This was before I was three years old; and soon after I recall trying to lift my little legs up a steep flight of stairs, which I never could identify afterward, until many years later I found they were the garret stairs in my great-grandfather's house, near Munt Hill.

My two great-grandmothers, neither of whom I ever saw, Anna Towle and Esther Towle (who were second cousins), seem to have introduced into the Sanborn and the Leavitt families the tall stature and great strength that distinguished some of their descendants. Anna Towle, the widow of Benjamin Sanborn, owned this old house near Munt Hill (a ledge celebrated in tradition as the occasional home of an Indian chief), and her gigantic son John lived in a cottage near by. A younger son, Jeremy, his mother's darling, died at nineteen, in her house (1786), and she is said never to have sat at her table with the household afterward, though she lived until 1823, when she must have been ninety years old. Her young son's tall clock then fell to his brother, my grandfather, and still ticks the solemn time in the "clock-room" of the house where I was born—the large room where in winter we dined, and where I studied Latin, French, Greek, and German, before I ever thought of going to Harvard College. The facilities for so many languages were furnished by what remained of the church library "for the use of the Ministry," given by Dr. Langdon, the parish clergyman, a retired president of Harvard; and by the text-books which my brother Charles bought for his own studies. Dr. Langdon's meeting-house was near by, on what was originally a town-common and parade-ground, and earlier a garrison palisade, with a schoolhouse near the garrison, in the time of Indian dangers. The meeting-house was built shortly before the Revolution, and in its loft were kept the military stores for that and the next English war. The Parsonage stood cornering on another little common, in front of my grandfather's house, and Dr. Langdon and Parson Abbot, his successor, were the nearest neighbors of my ancestors from 1780, when Dr. Langdon indignantly withdrew from his insulted presidency, until 1827, when Mr. Abbot retired to his hill-farm in Windham, twenty miles inland. In this half-century (almost) the foundation of a reading and studious community was laid in my native township; both these clergymen being learned scholars, fond of disseminating culture among their parishioners. Both founded local libraries—Dr. Langdon of Latin, Greek and historical folios, quartos, octavos, and pamphlets; and Parson Abbot a "social" lending library wholly in English, and more popular in its quality. Both were customarily kept in the Parsonage, and were open to me, a schoolmate of the sons of successive parsons, and their playmate on the little triangular common where the Exeter road, Hampton old-road and Kensington crossroad came together. From this Social library, of which my father was a shareholder, I borrowed and read "Plutarch's Lives" (Langhorne's translation) before I was eight years old, and had read most of its few hundred books before beginning, at about fourteen, to read the Langdon volumes. At the age of eleven a lively young schoolmaster, Barber, of Epping, induced me to begin the Greek grammar, and I had learned the alphabet and the first paradigms when my father sent word to my teacher that I was too young for that study. I was already entered in Latin, and read along by myself for several years in *Liber Primus,* Nepos, the "Colloquies of Erasmus" (of which, as well as of Terence, I found a copy in the Langdon library), and Virgil. I took up Greek again in 1846, at the age of fifteen or earlier, and have never given it up since.

My religious education was hardly so early and continuous as my literary studies. My grandparents in both families, and their fathers, had been loyal parishioners of Dr. Langdon; but after his death, in 1797, although, from our own house, so near the church, the family went to meeting in the old way, my Grandfather Leavitt, the Jeffersonian justice of the peace, more for political than spiritual reasons, I fancy, joined the seceding Baptists, and refused to pay his church-rates, which were then assessed by the town. This led to his arrest, and made him more a political leader than before; for while the Congregationalists or the "standing

THE SANBORN HOUSEHOLD, 1868

On the Croquet Ground, Hampton Falls

The Figures (from left to right) are Sarah and Helen, Mrs. Lydia Sanborn, Miss Hannah Leavitt, a niece of Mrs. S., Mrs. F. B. Sanborn, with her son Thomas and his cousin Mary Sanborn, the doctor's child.

order " were generally Federalists, the sects (Baptists, Methodists, etc.) were apt to be Jeffersonian Republicans. Squire Tom's first commission as justice was given him by John Langdon, the Jeffersonian leader in New Hampshire, and he was proud of that honor. Every succeeding Governor renewed the commission, until my grandfather's death, in 1852; and he continued to be a Democratic leader in Rockingham County until the party hopelessly divided on the issue of Texas annexation, in 1844-5. Meanwhile he had left the Baptists, who were Calvinists, and organized a small Universalist society in Hampton Falls, of which my father (his son-in-law) and his brother, Joseph Sanborn, were members, and which their father, " Grandsir Sanborn," good-naturedly joined, having already given up his Federalist politics and followed Adams, at first, and then Jackson, into the reorganized Democracy, in 1828-30. These Universalists never settled a pastor, but had preaching in schoolhouses and private parlors for a few years, set up a theological library, the books of which were soon distributed among the faithful; and eventually, about 1838, became Unitarians, under the pastorates of Rev. Stephen Farley, Rev. Linus Shaw, and Rev. Jacob Caldwell, all successors in the old parsonage of Langdon and Abbot. But neither of my grandfathers, nor my father and his brother, went often to church, although the women of their families did; and it was not required of me, as a child, to go regularly, or to attend the Sunday school. I read the Univer-

salist and Unitarian books, was familiar with the
Bible, and at the mature age of nine, after reading
how Origen and other Greek fathers believed in
final salvation for all, I declared myself a Universalist. I believe I never heard a Universalist
preacher until I entered college, but took up the
habit of going among the Baptists, the Congregationalists, and others, wherever there was good
preaching and singing. This wandering habit continued until the more advanced type of Unitarians
attracted my attention—Wentworth Higginson,
James Richardson, Horatio Wood and A. A. Liv-
ermore (both sons-in-law of Parson Abbot), and
James Freeman Clarke—and I became a constant
reader of Mr. Clarke's *Christian World,* a Boston
weekly that still seems to me the best religious
newspaper Boston issued in my time—too good, in
fact, to be long supported.

This brings me to my sixteenth year, when my
literary career may be said to have fairly begun.
In mature life I have had, in a humble way, four
distinct careers—political, literary, socially reformatory, and journalistic or publicist. Of these,
the political was first developed, and then the literary.

In a democracy like ours (and New Hampshire
in my boyhood was more nearly a pure democracy
than any region, not excepting modern Greece,
which I have since visited) it is singular how early
the political instinct is developed and stimulated.
My relatives (except my Boston uncles, who had
become Whigs) being all Democrats, I was natu-

rally of that partisan faith as early as eight years
old. Isaac Hill's *New Hampshire Patriot* had
been taken by my father before I was born, and
the old numbers remained stored up in the garret,
along with almanacs and *New Hampshire Regis-
ters* as far back as 1800; these feasted my eager
appetite for political fact and fiction. About 1840
the weekly edition of the Boston *Post* came in, a
brilliant and unprincipled journal, very entertain-
ing to a boy. On the other side was the mild Exeter
News-Letter, anti-Democratic, and an occasional
Portsmouth *Journal,* Boston *Mercantile Journal*
and other Whig newspapers, which the clergy and
wealthier farmers and merchants, and my own
Whig uncles, took, who sent copies to their trenchant Democratic father, the old Squire. At his
house and at our own, when he came there, as he
often did, I heard the Jackson and Van Buren and
Marcus Morton gospel of Democracy set forth in
conversation; and at school the boys took sides vig-
orously in the campaigns. When General Harri-
son was running against Van Buren in 1840, I had
a bet of fourpence-happeny (6¼ cents) pending
with Henry Shaw, the son of our neighbor, the
parson—I going on nine, and he two years older.
Of course I lost, although my State (of this I
was very proud) stood loyally by "Little Van, the
Used-up Man," as Henry termed the august President. Little did we know of the principles involved—but were illustrating a maxim of my
Grandsir Sanborn, "As the old cock crows, the
young 'un larns." Two years later I was deeply

interested in the Dorr Rebellion in Rhode Island, and took great pleasure in the schism of the victorious Whig party, occasioned by Clay's imperious demand and President Tyler's rather absurd resistance; taking my cue, of course, from the Boston *Post*. But soon there came a change o'er the spirit of my dream. The invincible New Hampshire Democrats themselves quarreled, and in 1844 our brilliant Congressman, Hale, of Dover, refused to go with the majority of his party for the annexation of Texas, which (under the sophistical name of " Re-annexation ") had become the party shibboleth. Polk was elected President upon that issue, after Van Buren had been refused a renomination because he opposed annexation. So had the New Hampshire Democrats done in 1843; but slavery demanded new territory, and the leaders of the party in New Hampshire—Franklin Pierce, Moses Norris and Levi Woodbury—resolved that Hale should be disciplined for his independence. He had received a renomination to Congress for the Rockingham and Strafford section of the State— all that was New Hampshire for the first century of its colonization—but Pierce traversed the counties, demanding that a new nomination should be made, and an insignificant citizen, John Woodbury, was put on the general ticket for Congress. The State had not then been districted, and the whole body of voters decided that Woodbury must not succeed Hale. Our section went unrepresented until a friend of Hale, Tuck of Exeter, was elected two years later, Hale having been chosen Senator in 1846. This apparently trifling contest was the germ of great events, for Hale was the first Senator chosen on a distinct anti-slavery platform; and the revolt in the New Hampshire Democracy prefigured the general reorganization of parties in 1856.

At the time of Hale's separation from his party I was just thirteen, but had been a reader and student of politics for some years. My elder brother, Charles, was twenty-three, and became a local leader in our section among the "Independent Democrats," as the new party was called. I joined it with him, though it was still eight years before I was entitled by age to vote. This introduced a political schism in both branches of our family, the Sanborns and the Leavitts. My father and grandfathers remained in the old Democratic party, while my uncles in Boston, Benson and Joseph Leavitt, had become Whigs, and Benson was at the time senior alderman of Boston on the Whig side. Two of my father's sons and three of my grandfather's grandsons joined the new party; while my mother's cousins, Norris, the Congressman, afterward Senator, and the Leavitts of Pittsfield, were active in the pro-slavery Democracy. The schism was never healed, and it was the occasion of much grief and some anger to my father to see his sons arrayed against him and his party at elections. In time, the Boston alderman also became warm in his opposition to the anti-slavery party; so that neither at home nor when I visited Boston did I find sympathy with my opinions among my elders.

This did not shake my youthful enthusiasm in the least. I had joined the party of youth, and among my schoolmates and younger friends, and in their families, there was much encouragement for my growing sentiments. The few clergymen whom I met were also apt to be anti-slavery men, but I do not recall that I ever heard an abolition orator until the spring of 1851, when I spent a week in Boston, and listened to Theodore Parker and Wendell Phillips. I had read their speeches and sermons assiduously, however, in the newspapers that came to hand, and I was much versed in Congressional debates, then well reported in the *Congressional Globe,* to which my brother was a subscriber. He was also an assistant editor for a while of the weekly *Independent Democrat,* which I read constantly, from its establishment in 1845-6 by my brother's friend, George Fogg, afterward minister to Switzerland and Senator. It was the organ of the new party in New Hampshire, was very well edited, though with some personal bitterness (very much in fashion among New Hampshire partisans), and was the first periodical to which I contributed in print. This journal long since ceased to exist, and files of it can scarcely be found; it had much influence, however, in determining the politics of my native State from 1845 until the death of Abraham Lincoln, of whom its editor became an intimate friend during the presidential campaign of 1860.

Mr. Fogg was secretary of the National Republican Committee in that momentous contest, and had much to do with throwing the vote of New Hampshire for Lincoln in the Chicago convention which nominated him. Indeed, the New Hampshire Republicans in 1859 invited Mr. Lincoln to speak in their State election contest of that year, and I have heard Mr. Fogg tell with animation how the feelings of the State Committee at Concord changed from depression to enthusiasm as Lincoln began and continued his one speech there. New Hampshire had seen many stoutly contested annual elections, and our friends there had heard all the good orators on both sides; but they had never heard Lincoln. His first appearance was not prepossessing, and when Mr. Fogg escorted him to the platform, and listened to his halting and awkward first sentences, his heart sank within him. Just then he was called out upon some business of the committee, and when he returned to the hall, after a few minutes, entered by another door. He could scarcely trust his eyes when he saw this hesitating and almost grotesque speaker commanding the audience by his tones and his gestures, and holding them as completely in his power as the graceful Phillips or the majestic Webster could have done. That evening decided the votes of New Hampshire for Lincoln, when it was found that Seward could not unite the party as its candidate. So assured was Senator Seward that he would receive the nomination that about the middle of May, 1860, when the Chicago convention was assembling, he withdrew from the Senate and returned home to Auburn, N. Y., there to receive the expected notification. As he was leaving, he reproached our Massachusetts Senator, Wilson, for not favoring his presidential aspirations, saying, "You have done more against my nomination than any member of the Senate." But the first two ballots showed that Seward was wrong and Wilson right; and on the third ballot Lincoln was nominated.

During Senator Fogg's last illness, in which he lingered for some months, his old friend, Frank Bird, of Walpole, and I went up to visit him in his bachelor's home at Concord, N. H. He spoke with some difficulty, though in full possession of his memory and sagacity, and he was specially anxious to tell us an anecdote of President Lincoln and Senator Seward, of which he seems to have been the only relater. Lincoln had arrived in Washington, safe from the plot to assassinate him in Maryland, and was making up his cabinet. His wish was to place in it both Mr. Seward and Judge Chase. To the latter Mr. Seward strenuously objected, through his ancient friend and oracle, Thurlow Weed. The argument against Chase was fully presented, and finally Mr. Seward declared, by Mr. Weed, that he could not accept an appointment in the same cabinet with Judge Chase. Mr. Lincoln took the case under advisement. The next morning he met Mr. Fogg, who, as secretary of the campaign committee, had won his confidence, and told him the situation. Then, with a twinkle in his eye, he added, "We must give up both Seward and Chase, I reckon; and I have drawn up here a list of the cabinet, leaving them both out."

Handing the list to Mr. Fogg, the latter read, with surprise and amusement,

" Secretary of State, William L. Dayton of New Jersey;
Secretary of War, John C. Frémont of California;
Secretary of the Treasury (a New Yorker unfriendly
  to Seward)

and so on. "I am sending this to Mr. Weed," said Mr. Lincoln. The effect was what both had of course anticipated; when Mr. Seward found that a cabinet was planned in which he could have no personal influence, he intimated that he withdrew his objection to Mr. Chase, and both were appointed, as the President had intended from the first. Indeed, when Mr. Lincoln in the December before had been visited at Springfield by Thurlow Weed, and the names of Seward and Chase were mentioned to him, it does not appear that Weed took any objection to their joint appointment— the men to whom Mr. Weed objected being Cameron and Montgomery Blair. The attempt to eliminate Chase must, therefore, have been Seward's own motion, and was in the line with his later offer in writing, to Mr. Lincoln, that he would direct, as Secretary of State, the policy of the new administration: a proposal to which the President gave a prompt and sufficient negative.

But I am far in advance of my story; for I never saw either Lincoln or Seward. Judge Chase I had known before the war, meeting him at Theodore Parker's in 1858. I saw him last at the Dartmouth College Centennial of 1869, at the house

of Professor Sanborn, the father of my faraway
cousin, Miss Kate Sanborn, and then I noticed that
quivering of the features that indicated how near
was the paralysis which ended his eminent career.*
He was in his aspect one of the stateliest public
men of his time, and himself a New Hampshire
man, like Webster, Greeley, Henry Wilson and
Judge Woodbury, his contemporaries, though several of them older than himself. I co-operated
with Mr. Bird and our associates of the Boston
Bird Club in giving a public dinner to Mr. Chase
when leaving the Treasury Department in 1864.

When I began to continue Greek studies more
systematically, in 1850, in preparation for college,
I took lessons for a year from Prof. J. G. Hoyt,
of Exeter, an accomplished graduate of Dartmouth, and a teacher in the Phillips Exeter Academy. He was also an ardent anti-slavery man and
active in the politics of New Hampshire; and by
him I was introduced, in 1851, to his townsmen,
James Bell, for a short time Senator in Congress,
and to Amos Tuck, the Independent Democratic
Congressman who succeeded John Parker Hale.
Entering the old Academy a year later, in November, 1851, I was fitted to enter Harvard College in
July, 1852, a year in advance, and joined the sopho-
more class at Cambridge in September. I was still
under age, but a pronounced member of the party
organized by Senator Hale and his friends in 1845,
and a warm opponent of Hale's and Hawthorne's
Bowdoin College friend, Pierce, then the success-

*He was stricken in 1870 and died in 1880.

ful candidate of the pro-slavery Democrats for
President. I had seen Pierce and heard him argue
a criminal case in the Exeter Court House, ten
years before, but had no acquaintance with him,
nor with my second cousin, Norris, then Senator
with Hale from New Hampshire, whom I had
merely seen at my mother's house years before. My
personal acquaintance was indeed quite limited, as
my travels had been.

A few visits to Newburyport and Portsmouth,
the largest towns in my region, three visits to Boston among my relatives, an early trip with my
father to his cattle pasture in Pittsfield, and a walking tour to the White Mountains and the upper
valley of the Connecticut, returning through Leb-
anon, Concord and Northwood, in the year 1850—
such was the range of my travels at the age of
nineteen. But in the political field I had traveled
far, and was reasonably familiar with the different
parties and the character of their leaders. I had
even seen two Presidents, actual and prospective,
in one barouche at Portsmouth—Polk, making his
presidential tour in 1846, with Buchanan, his Secretary of State, and slowly driving along a Portsmouth street, near the residence of Judge Woodbury, who, but for the serious fact of his death,
was to have been the New Hampshire President in
1853, instead of General Pierce. His nomination
and election were assured, had he not died in September, 1851, after ranking for five or six years
among the eminent justices of the national Supreme Court, to which place he was appointed by

President Polk in 1845. Between Polk and Pierce came the broken administration of General Taylor, followed by Vice-President Fillmore, in whose time, and during the later years of Webster, the last of Henry Clay's compromises, the so-called "finality" measures of 1850, intended to quiet forever the agitation against negro slavery, were enacted, and the Union was "saved" for the third or fourth time.

All the political literature of the dismal years of the Mexican War and the territorial agitations that followed were well known to me in specimens—for nobody could possibly read it all; and my mind was fully made up on the main question. That slavery was wrong, that we of the North were governed by a minority small in numbers but powerful in wealth and influence, made up of the slaveholders and their commercial and manufacturing allies at the North and West, and that the mass of the people must free themselves from this dominating aristocracy, were truths that appealed to my naturally democratic sentiments so early that I hardly remember when I thought otherwise. Yet I never gave in to the doctrine of the Garrisonians that the Union established by our fathers should be given up; although at times it seemed as if only in that way could the evil institution of slavery be thrown off. I was instinctively of the faith that our national Constitution was an anti-slavery document, as Gerrit Smith and John Brown declared—and as in fact it proved to be, when the revolt of the slave States forced upon the nation the alternative of emancipation or the destruction of national existence.

Although this was the turn of my mind, it was, of course, only gradually that I came to clear ideas on the subject. These ideas were much promoted by two or three strong influences. One was the *National Era,* a weekly journal published at Washington, in which Whittier, Mrs. Stowe, and other good writers maintained the attitude of the voting emancipationists; another was Horace Greeley's *Tribune,* which, while adhering to the Whig party as long as it could, yet dealt the most trenchant blows at the monster of misgovernment which then controlled affairs in the United States. Another influence, and in my case the strongest, was the tenor of all good literature, of which I became very early and have long continued to be a general student. All literature worthy of the name is and must be on the side of freedom, though it may also be a maintainer of reasonable authority. For without freedom no good literature can be born or long exist. The poets are on the side of freedom, and the virtues and graces are so, too.

My way of life at home on the farm, and the studies I pursued, were such as to foster an original turn of thought. The labor I performed was not hard, nor oppressive in its continuance; it was often solitary labor in the field or the woods, leaving the mind free to entertain its own thoughts. So far as it was social, or performed in the company of others, it promoted conversation, and gave a ready mind access to all that store of homely wit and natural fact which was put to such wonderful use by Abraham Lincoln, who picked it up, as I did in a smaller way, by listening to the talk and noticing the ways of the countryside. Following the mowers in the hay-field, or sitting with parents and brothers and neighbors under an apple tree in summer, or beside a fire of boughs in the winter grove, what snatches of wit and wisdom have I not heard! Grinding scythes, repairing roads, making shoes or tools in the little shops, the best part of unconscious education may be acquired from the remarks made and pondered, the debates carried on, and the anecdotes related. I was never very shy or unsocial, made friends easily, and was tolerated or praised by my elders, and never thought myself, so far as I remember, the most important person in any company, large or small, where I found myself. A husking-party, a game of checkers or of cards, a stroll in the pastures with young comrades, bearing guns and enlivened by dogs, tea parties and school examinations and evening debates in the district schoolhouse—such and a hundred other occasions for learning and practicing social good humor and the untaught lore of human nature, formed my character, such as it is, and made me, I dare say, a fair representative of myriads of my New England countrymen. In one thing I perhaps differed—in freedom from avarice or ambition. I never yearned for great wealth, nor sought for leadership or high place in the world; such leadership as I may have had (and most men of education take the lead in something) must have

come from character, not from ambition. But
along with this contentment in the station I have
had went a firm resolve not to be domineered over
by others, either individuals or classes; and I saw
no reason why I should take my opinions from the
majority, or the cultivated minority—or from any
source except my own much-considering mind. In
this, no doubt, there was a certain pride, to which
respectable sin rather than to the more common
quality of vanity it is likely I have been too much
inclined.

Changing my residence to Cambridge, I still
maintained my right to vote in my native town of
New Hampshire, where, under the old law, I "had
my washing and mending done"; and my first vote
was cast in March, 1853, at the State election following the inauguration of our only New Hampshire President, Pierce. He had received a majority of 6700 in 1852; his party the next spring
got but 5400, and in 1855, the last year I voted
there, the Democrats went out of power in New
Hampshire for twenty years. This was the response of his native State to the support given by
President Pierce to the extension of slavery, by
promoting the repeal of the Missouri Compromise,
in order to let slavery into Kansas. He made
a bad matter worse by following the lead of Jefferson Davis, his Secretary of War, and appointing
territorial officers who tried to force slavery in, thus
bringing on a state of civil war in Kansas. By
this time, 1855-6, I was out of college and a voting
citizen of Old Concord, as my town has been called

for a century and a quarter, to distinguish it from the dozen or twenty Concords in various parts of the United States—all named in honor of the skirmish by the Concord River which opened the war of the Revolution. The Kansas conflict gave me my first opportunity for important political activity, and brought me into friendship with one of the heroic historical figures of the last century, John Brown, of Kansas and Virginia.

CHAPTER II

National Politics—1854-1861

CAMBRIDGE, the seat of Harvard College, being in 1852, even more than now, a suburb and appendage of Boston, my residence there from September, 1852, to March, 1855, when I went to reside in Concord, gave me the opportunity of knowing the men who afterward had much to do with shaping the policy of the nation. In April, 1851, I had seen General Banks, whose statue has this year been set up on Beacon Hill, near where I first saw him. He was then Speaker of the Massachusetts House of Representatives—a small but striking-looking man, almost lost to my view (from the gallery) in the great chair, but with his long black hair and piercing eyes attracting notice, as he did wherever he appeared for many years. I saw him in his glory and in his decline—for in later years his memory failed, so that he hardly knew what he was saying, although his graceful manner and polite tone survived. The last conversation with him that I recall was at a luncheon in the Parker House, Boston, where I saw him and Mrs. Banks at a table for four, and joined them, thinking I might enliven by conversation the rather somber side of life then presented to a man who had been very successful. I introduced the subjects, and General Banks allowed me to do most of the talking, for he had fallen into a silence quite marked in contrast with his former readiness of speech, whether public or private. Mrs. Banks also listened and asked the needful questions, as I tried one topic after another in the hope of interesting the fading veteran. He seemed pleased, and responded here and there; but evidently he did not follow the talk very clearly. At last, turning to his wife, he said, in his magnificent voice, "My dear, this is a very agreeable gentleman; may I ask you what his name is?" I had talked with him a hundred times, and he had known me as well as he knew his neighbors in Waltham, where he lived for half a century in a modest house, with a large tract of land, which, as the city grew, became valuable for house lots and for a park, and by its sale kept him from that degree of poverty which might otherwise have been his lot. He had no skill in the saving of money, and his general's pension for years was his chief income.

No full memoir of General Banks has ever been published, although one or two campaign biographies of him as a candidate had a good sale—he figuring therein as "The Bobbin-Boy of Waltham." Both he and Mrs. Banks had been cotton-mill operatives in their youth—a very common resource of worthy maidens and young men who had their own way to make in the world. Their manners in after life would never have suggested so humble an employment, if there were any necessary connection between the manners and the early

occupation of distinguished persons, as plainly
there is none. Banks from the first had an air of
distinction, and an ambition which well became
him. He desired to be a popular orator, and for
this purpose he frequented every good actor and
every famous speaker, whatever the style of the
orator might be. He told me that he had seen on
the American stage that interesting English actor,
Bernard, whose description of General Washington in his later years at Mount Vernon is one of
the best we have of that truly great man. General
Banks had seen the book, and agreed with me that
it was an account of Washington that could not be
spared from the many which profess to picture the
man as he was. Bernard, from his profession, was
apt to notice and catch the impression of a person's
features and manner; and he also had an easy style
which expressed readily what he wished to convey.
As the account, though reprinted in America, does
not seem to be widely known, I copy below its essential portions. General Banks is the only person
I have met who had seen Bernard on the stage; he
was not a great actor, but a natural and pleasing
one. As Banks was not born until January, 1816,
and Bernard died in 1828, it must have been early
in life that Banks saw him.

John Bernard says, as reported by his son, Bayle
Bernard: *

"In July, 1798, I had been to visit an acquaintance
on the banks of the Potomac, a few miles below Alex-

* *Retrospections of America,* 1797-1811. By John Bernard, New
York, Harper and Brothers, 1887. (Pp. 85-91.)

andria, and was returning on horseback, in the rear of
an old-fashioned chaise, the driver of which was urging
on his steed, when a lash, directed with more skill than
humanity, took the skin from an old wound. The sudden
pang threw the poor animal on his hind-legs, and, the
wheel swerving upon a bank, over went the chaise, fling-
ing out upon the road a young woman. The minute
before I had perceived a horseman approaching at a
gentle trot, who now broke into a gallop, and we reached
the scene of the disaster together. The female was our
first care; she was insensible, but had sustained no material injury. My companion supported her, while I
brought some water in the crown of my hat from a spring
some way off. The driver had landed on his legs, and
having ascertained that his spouse was not dead, seemed
well satisfied with the care she was in, and set about ex-
tricating his horse. A gush of tears announced the return of the lady to sensibility; then, as her eyes opened,
her tongue gradually resumed its office, as she poured
forth a volley of invectives on her mate.

"The horse was now on his legs, but the vehicle still
prostrate, heavy in its frame and laden with half a ton
of luggage. My fellow-helper set me an example of activity in relieving it of the external weight, and, when
all was clear, we grasped the wheel between us, and
righted the conveyance. The horse was then put in, and
we lent a hand to help up the luggage. All this helping,
hauling and lifting occupied at least half an hour, under
a meridian sun in the middle of July. Our unfortunate
friend somewhat relieved the task with his narrative. He
was a New Englander who had emigrated to the South
young, there picked up a wife and some money, and was
now on his way home, having been 'made very comfortable' by the death of his father. When all was right,

and we had assisted the lady to resume her seat, he begged us to proceed with him to Alexandria and take a drop of ' something sociable.' Finding that we were unsociable, he extended his hand, gripped ours as he had the heavy boxes, and, when we had sufficiently *felt* that he was grateful, drove on.

" My companion, after an exclamation at the heat, offered very courteously to dust my coat—a favor, the return of which enabled me to take a survey of his person. He was a tall, erect, well-made man, evidently advanced in years, but appeared to have retained all the vigor and elasticity resulting from a life of temperance and exercise. His dress was a blue coat buttoned to the chin, and buckskin breeches. Though, the instant he took off his hat, I could not avoid the recognition of familiar lineaments, still I failed to identify him; and, to my surprise, I found myself an object of equal speculation in his eyes. A smile at length lighted them up, and he exclaimed, ' Mr. Bernard, I believe.' I bowed. ' I had the pleasure of seeing you perform last winter in Philadelphia.' I bowed again, and he added, ' I have heard of you since from several of my friends at Annapolis. You are acquainted with Mr. Carroll? ' I replied that gentleman's society had made amends for much that I had lost in quitting England. He remarked, ' You must be fatigued. If you will ride up to my house, which is not a mile distant, you can prevent any ill effects from this exertion by a couple of hours' rest.' I looked round for his dwelling, and he pointed to a building which, the day before, I had spent an hour in contemplating. ' Mount Vernon! ' I exclaimed; and then, drawing back with a stare of wonder—' Have I the honor of addressing General Washington? ' With a smile, whose expression of benevolence I have rarely seen equaled, he offered his

hand and replied, ' An odd sort of introduction, Mr.
Bernard; but I am pleased to find you can play so active
a part in private, and without a prompter.' I needed
no further stimulus to accept his friendly invitation. As
we rode up to his house, we entered freely into conversation.

" Flattering as his inquiries were, from such a source
(respecting my success in America, and my impressions
of the country) my own reflections on what had just
passed were more absorbing. Nine ordinary country gentlemen out of ten who had seen a chaise upset near their
estate, would have thought it savored neither of pride
nor ill-nature to ride home and send servants to its assistance. But I had witnessed one of the strongest evi-
dences of a great man's claim to his reputation—the
prompt, impulsive working of a heart which, having made
the good of mankind its religion, was never so happy as
in practically displaying it. On reaching the house we
found that Mrs. Washington was indisposed; but the
General ordered refreshments in a parlor whose windows
took a noble range of the Potomac, and, after a few
minutes' absence, rejoined me.

" Whether you surveyed Washington's face, open, yet
well defined, dignified, but not arrogant, thoughtful, but
benign; his frame, towering and muscular, but alert from
its good proportion—every feature suggested a re-
semblance to the spirit it encased, and showed simplicity
in alliance with the sublime. The impression was that
of a most perfect whole, something sacred as well as
wonderful; a man fashioned by the hand of Heaven with
every requisite to achieve a great work. Thus a feeling
of awe and veneration stole over you. In conversation
his face had not much variety of expression. A look of
thoughtfulness was given by the compression of the mouth

and the indentation of the brow, which did not seem so
much to disdain a sympathy with trivialities, as to be incapable of denoting them. Nor had his voice, so far as
I could discover in our quiet talk, much change or rich-
ness of intonation; but he always spoke with earnestness,
and his eyes, glorious conductors of the light within,
burned with a steady fire which no one could mistake for
mere affability. He spoke like a man who had felt as
much as he had reflected, and reflected more than he had
spoken. He touched on every topic that I brought before
him with an even current of good sense, if he embellished
it with little wit or verbal elegance. When I mentioned
to him the difference I perceived between the people of
New England and of the South, he remarked, ' I esteem
those people greatly; they are the stamina of the Union,
and its greatest benefactors. They are continually
spreading themselves, too—to settle and enlighten less
favored quarters. Dr. Franklin was a New Englander.'
He added, ' I consider England the cradle of free principles, not their arm-chair; liberty there is a sort of idol—
people there are bred up in the belief and love of it, but
see little of its doings. They walk about freely, but it is
within high walls; and the error of its government was
to suppose that, after a portion of its subjects had
crossed the sea to live upon a common, they would permit
their friends at home to build up those walls about them.'

" He considered the dramatic stage to be an indispensable resource for settled society, and a chief refiner; not
merely interesting as a comment on social happiness by
its exhibition of manners, but an agent of good as a
school for poetry, holding up to honor the noblest principles. ' I am too old and too far removed to seek for or
require this pleasure myself, but the cause is not to droop
on my account. There's my friend, Mr. Jefferson, has

time and taste; he goes always to the play, and I'll introduce you to him.' A promise which he kept, and which proved to me a source of the greatest benefit and pleasure."

General Banks was himself an actor in his youthful days, and might have risen to some eminence in that profession if politics had not drawn him aside. He thought John Bernard a fairly good actor, as he surely was a good observer and a pleasing writer. Few have better described the essential character of Washington, as seen in his vigorous age.

When Banks mentioned the Bernard incident to me his remarkable memory had not given way, and it was by virtue of that, rather than by anything original or profound in his thought, that he became a popular orator; but he had the fortune to make a deep impression on those who heard him for the first time; and he retained his popularity through many changes of circumstance and opinion. He entered the Massachusetts Legislature in 1840, and he did not leave Congress till 1890. He was Governor in 1858-59 and 1860.

In his governorship and in his military life, General Banks did not acquire a permanent fame; but it is likely that he was judged unfairly in both positions. His early connection with the disreputable Native American or " Know-Nothing " party brought about him as Governor associates who had not the confidence of men in established position, but were viewed as shifty adventurers. But he had also attached friends of a different class, and there was not much fault to find with his measures while Governor. One of them in the year 1859 became famous, and was of service in the Civil War that soon followed—his State muster of the volunteer militia at Concord, in the plain long since chiefly occupied by the State Reformatory, along the Assabet River. It furnished a fine spectacle, and one of its brave sights was Governor Banks himself, mounted on a black thoroughbred horse, reviewing the troops, among whom was General B. F. Butler, then a major-general of militia. Banks was Governor also when the present King of England, then Prince of Wales, was officially received in Boston; and in the ceremonies then obligatory, Banks bore his part well. I saw the Prince in the street near the old Fitchburg Station in Boston, surrounded by his escort and the crowd—a slender, fair youth of eighteen, not handsome, but winning and amiable, as he has since shown himself in his public capacity.

On leaving the governorship at the beginning of 1860, Banks introduced the custom of a valedictory address, for which his opponents (of whom I was then and afterward one) did not see so much occasion as he did. Coming home in the train that night, after reading the address, I asked my neighbor, Judge Hoar, elder brother of the Senator: "Why did Governor Banks think it necessary to make this address?" The Judge smiled sardonically and said: "I suppose for the same reason that the boy's father whipped him. Johnny was out playing with other boys, when a vigorous rapping on the window by his father called him indoors. Soon after he came out again, weeping and rubbing himself. 'Did he lick ye? did he lick ye?' said the sympathizing gang. 'He did; oh, he did!' 'What for?' 'For his own glory, I suppose.' And that," said Judge Hoar, "was the reason of the Governor's oratory to-day."

Such was the way we were in the habit of joking about His Excellency in those days. When Thoreau, who lived in Concord, near the railroad station where the Governor and his friends might alight in the days of the great Muster, was going down to the post office one of those days, he was met by a neighbor, who said, "Henry, where are you going?" "I heard that the Governor of Massachusetts is coming to Concord to-day, and I am after a lock to put on our front door." "Yes, but the General Court is coming up, too." "Oh, then I must put a lock on our back door."

I have dwelt thus at some length on General Banks because he was the first of many Governors that I have known in the time of their reign, though I afterward knew several of his predecessors intimately—especially Governor Boutwell and Governor Emory Washburn—the latter denied a reelection by the swelling of the Know-Nothing tide in 1854. When the new legislators came up to take the oath of office early in 1855, most of them being new and unknown persons, that had supplanted men of experience who formerly came to the General Court, Governor Washburn is said to have remarked, after the oaths had all been taken, "You are now qualified, gentlemen—so far as taking the oath of office can qualify you, to sit as members of the General Court." To which the Secretary of State added the usual chorus, " God save the Commonwealth of Massachusetts! "

So much for N. P. Banks, Speaker, Congressman, Governor and Major-General, suggested by my sight of him in April, 1851, sitting in the Speaker's chair. In the same month I heard Theodore Parker and Wendell Phillips—the former in his famous Fast-day sermon after the return of Sims, the fugitive, to slavery, delivered April 10, 1851. I did not then have the honor of his acquaintance, and my uncle, the ex-alderman and acting Mayor of 1845, whom I was visiting, was aggrieved that I went to hear Parker, concerning whom he had the common Whig opinion—that he was infidel and disorganizing, and was "resisting the government." In July, 1852, while waiting for my college examination to be concluded, I went from this uncle's house in Charter Street across the way to the house of Rev. Edward Beecher, then preaching at the North End of Boston, to call on Mrs. Stowe, whom I there saw for the first time. She was in the height of her fame as the author of " Uncle Tom's Cabin," one of the epoch-making books of the nineteenth century, which, after coming out in Dr. Bailey's *National Era* at Washington in 1851-2, was published in Boston by Jewett and sold more than a quarter-million copies. She was a plain, affectionate and simple person in 1852,

and I was interested to see the terms she was on
with her youngest brother James, then living in or
near Boston, and whom I afterward knew under
very different circumstances. Later in the year
1852 I was introduced by my friend Miss Ednah
Littlehale, afterward the wife of Seth Cheney, the
delicate crayon artist, to the Alcott family, then
living in Pinckney Street, Boston, and saw for the
first time Louisa Alcott, who now has a wider audience for her lively and pathetic fiction than even
Mrs. Stowe had half a century ago. It was in this
eventful year also that I became the friend of
Theodore Parker, with whom I was afterward
much associated, and whose manuscripts are now
my property by the bequest of his wife. I was his
executor, along with Messrs. May and Manly, in
1860, and was selected by him as his posthumous
editor—a task which I could not undertake for
reasons I may give hereafter. In 1853 I heard
Charles Sumner for the first time, in Faneuil Hall,
and before then had become intimate with Dr. S.
G. Howe, whose life by his daughter, Mrs. Rich-
ards, is this year completed. I had heard Colonel
Higginson preach in my native town while he had
a parish in Newburyport, and I made his personal
acquaintance in 1853. I had called on Whittier in
his cottage at Amesbury, and had heard Longfel-
low lecture in Harvard College. In this same year,
1853, in early July, I called on Emerson at Concord, and became a frequent hearer of his inspir-
ing lectures. Thus the circle of my political and
literary friends was formed in good part during

my first two years in college, and when I had lately reached the age of one and twenty. To these friends many more were added as the next few years went by; but I lost that invaluable and beloved friend, Miss Walker, of whom more will be said in my literary recollections. Her death occurred in August, 1854, while the country was in the midst of the agitation occasioned by the repeal of the Missouri Compromise, and the seizure of fugitive slaves under the wicked enactment of 1850, in which Webster had concurred. Webster, with that fatal weakness of character which contrasted forcibly with the native strength of his understanding, had fallen away from the lofty positions he had early and often taken against the existence, and still more, the extension, of negro slavery; had made his evil 7th of March speech in 1850, and had died in October, 1852, before he was able to cast his vote for a pro-slavery President from his native State. The evil he had done lived after him, and contributed something to the wicked effort of that New Hampshire President to force slavery into new territory which, by the Missouri Compromise, had been consecrated to free labor. In view of this very piece of infamy, Webster had said, in 1845, when resisting the annexation of Texas: " The theory that the Constitution of 1787 was made for the preservation, encouragement and expansion of slavery dates its discovery from a period long subsequent to the establishment of the government." That false theory, he went on to say:

" Declares that every new acquisition which Freedom shall make on her own soil, through the blessings of Heaven upon toil and enterprise, should be counterbalanced by the incorporation into the body politic of an equal portion of exotic slavery; and that the decline of such slavery through the operation of beneficent causes should be retarded by subjecting to its desolating influence new regions, acquired by purchase or fraud or force."

The practical issue of the enforcement of this malign theory of Calhoun and the Southern slavemasters by President Pierce, through Atchison of Missouri, Douglas of Illinois and Jefferson Davis, the residuary legatee of Calhoun's heresies, was in 1854 the source of unavoidable civil war. It depended on the people of the North to say whether they would, in the words of Webster, "uphold the interests of slavery, extend its influence, and secure its permanent duration," or whether the majority of the people of the United States, at the expense even of much blood and treasure (as in the Civil War), should carry out that professed object of the Constitution of Washington and Franklin, "To establish justice, insure domestic tranquillity, provide for the common defense, promote the general welfare, and secure the blessings of *liberty* to themselves and their posterity." These were the great interests really at stake in the political contests from 1854 to 1861, and in the Kansas campaigns of 1856-58. Feeling this as warmly and foreseeing it as clearly in 1854 as it is now visible in retrospect, and aided in this clearness of

insight by the remarkable political wisdom of Theodore Parker, I announced such opinions in one of
my college declamations, and acted upon them
steadily thereafter. I had the advantage of hearing, at the evening receptions of Parker in his open
house on Exeter Place, both sides of the controversy, and all its varying phases, discussed by
emancipationists and slaveholders, by followers of
Webster in his change of sentiment, and by the laconic and trenchant conversation of John Brown.
Removing to Concord early in 1855, I there found
the circle in which I moved holding much the same
sentiments, modified by peculiarities of age and
native character, in Samuel Hoar, father of the
Senator, who had been insulted in South Carolina
for maintaining the doctrines of the Constitution in
that slave-trading region; in Emerson, the calm ad-
vocate of principles, and Thoreau, who went a step
farther in his theories of government and society;
and in Judge Hoar, who, without his father's courtesy and equity, had a pungency of wit and a power
of indignation which made him a tower of strength
in any cause that he took up. It was he who inserted in the Republican platform of 1856 the
striking phrase, "those twin relics of barbarism,
polygamy and slavery"; and he had already, on his
judicial bench, asserted the right of a people to
disobey wicked laws, holding, with Jefferson, that
there are "sacred and sovereign rights reserved in
the hands of the people for cases of extreme necessity, and judged by the Constitution (of England)
unsafe to be delegated to any other judicature."

He also believed in the doctrine laid down by Webster in January, 1845:

> "That government is a delegated and limited trust; that all authority not conferred is reserved; and that, in fact, there are grave questions, lying deeper than the ordinary forms of government, and over which government, in none of its branches, has just control."

This statement could have been accepted by Thoreau, and it was, in fact, the political theory of John Brown. It asserts the right and duty of revolution, and is the only theory upon which American independence could be maintained in 1776. Josiah Quincy the elder, then in his ninety-second year, wrote to Judge Hoar in May, 1856, in the same revolutionary tenor with his father, the patriot of 1774:

> (May 27.) "I can think of nothing but the outrages of slaveholders at Kansas, and the outrages of slaveholders at Washington" (the brutal assault on Sumner in the Senate chamber); "outrages which, if not met in the spirit of our fathers of the Revolution (and I see no sign that they will be) our liberties are but a name, and our Union proves a curse. But alas! sir, I see no principle of vitality in what is called Freedom in these times. The palsy of death rests on the spirit of freedom in the so-called Free States."

The tone of Mr. Quincy's letter, but less despairing, as befitted younger men, was that of the whole circle in which I lived in 1856, including then at Boston, John A. Andrew, afterward our

DR. S. G. HOWE, 1855

War Governor; Frank Bird, founder of the Bird
Club, which I joined about 1854, and in which I
succeeded Mr. Bird (at his death in 1894) as president; also Sumner, Henry Wilson, Anson Bur-
lingame, Dr. Howe, William S. Robinson (better
known as "Warrington"), James Freeman
Clarke, John M. Forbes, and many more of some
distinction at the time and since. Among the most
active in this very month of May, 1856, were Dr.
Howe and George L. Stearns of Medford, with
Gerrit Smith of Peterboro, N. Y., and T. W. Higginson, then a clergyman at Worcester. I joined
in their movement to raise money and buy arms for
our oppressed friends, the Free-State pioneers in
Kansas; and I became secretary of the Town Committee of Concord, of the Middlesex County Committee, and finally, later in the year 1856, of the
State Kansas Committee, which continued in existence for several years and raised much money
for the cause that finally triumphed. These duties
gave me a great deal of travel during the va-
cations of my Concord School, or when, as in 1857,
I placed an assistant master in charge of its departments. Our County Committee had for chairman
John Nesmith, of Lowell, afterward Lieutenant-
Governor, and among its members were C. C. Esty,
afterward a member of Congress, and Charles
Hammond, a distinguished teacher of American
and Japanese students. As secretary I conducted
the correspondence, and also spent the first half of
my summer vacation (1856) in driving over half of
Middlesex County in a "one-horse shay" of the

kind celebrated by Dr. Holmes, to organize town committees and raise money for emigrants, arms and supplies. The result was that in February, 1857, when I reported our funds to the subscribers, we had raised $17,383 in money and supplies from a population of 195,000 then living in Middlesex, of which Concord gave $2,242 from a population of 2,251.

In what remained of my summer vacation, I set forth, in August, 1856, as an agent of the Massachusetts State Kansas Committee (of which I was afterward secretary for some years) on a tour of inspection and consultation, that took me across the prairie States of Indiana, Illinois and Iowa, and over the Missouri River into what was then the Territory of Nebraska. It was my first journey west of the Hudson River, and allowed me to see Niagara by the way, and for the first time. Five years later, in May, 1861, my Concord neighbor, Thoreau, made his first visit to Niagara, and his tour of the same prairie States, although he went but little west of the Mississippi, but turned northward, and explored a portion of Minnesota and Wisconsin.* My first considerable halt on this journey was at Chicago, then a city of but some 80,000 people, but the seat of the National Kansas Committee, at whose office I first met Horace White, then secretary of the executive committee of the national body, and Captain Webster, after-

* In 1906 I edited, from Thoreau's notes, what he had never had the health and time to transcribe, his account of this, his last considerable journey.

ward General Grant's chief of artillery in the
Army of the Tennessee. I next proceeded to Iowa
City, then the actual capital of Iowa, to see the
Adjutant-General of the State with regard to some
of the State muskets, which had been lent to settlers in Kansas for their protection against invaders
from Missouri, and which, I have since heard, were
never fully returned to the Iowa arsenal.

Thence I went to the home of the Governor of
Iowa, James Wilson Grimes, who lived in Burlington; and I had an interesting interview with him in
regard to Kansas and Iowa. He was a New Hampshire man, and had studied law with my father-in-
law, James Walker, of Peterboro, N. H. In
crossing the Mississippi to reach Burlington—for
there were then no bridges over any of the great
rivers of the West—I found on the steamer Rev.
Edward Beecher, whom I had last seen in Boston,
and who was going to preach at Burlington the
next day (Sunday). I took tea with Governor
Grimes that Sunday evening, and went with his
family to hear Dr. Beecher afterward. The next
day, Mr. Fitz-Henry Warren, a Massachusetts
man, having some office in the Burlington & Missouri Railroad, then building through Iowa, gave
me a free pass as far as the tracks were laid (to
Mount Pleasant, a few miles west), and I started
on my slow journey over the prairie roads to the
Missouri River. At Mount Pleasant I met one of
the brothers Eldridge, whose Free-State Hotel in
Lawrence, Kansas, had been cannonaded, ruined
and pillaged a few months earlier by a body of

Missourians, among whom was Senator Atchison, lately acting Vice-President of the United States. Mr. Eldridge, seeing that I was unarmed, and without an overcoat (which at that age I seldom wore, even in winter), lent me his Colt's revolver, loaded and capped, and a green and blue plaid shawl, under which I took some agreeable naps in my night-rides inside or outside the slow stage-coaches of that time and place.

In these filthy coaches, with all sorts of companions, and lodging at all kinds of stage taverns, at all hours of the night-arrival, I traversed the 400 miles between Mount Pleasant and Council Bluffs, in the hot August weather of that year, inspecting the land-route by which we were sending emigrants to Kansas, after the Missouri River was practically closed to them by the pro-slavery men of Missouri, who were resolved that Kansas should become a slave State. It was then a slave Territory, partially colonized by slaveholders from various parts of the South, bringing a few slaves with them, and expecting to bring or see brought a great many more. There were many incidents of this four-days' trip, novel and interesting to me at the time; of which the most novel was an encampment of 300 Mormon converts from Europe, on their way to the then new colony of Deseret in Utah. I had some conversation with these poor creatures, mostly of the lowest English classes, and with their shrewd and selfish American leaders. Very early in this singular Mormon movement, when Joe Smith, a Vermont bricklayer, was its chief leader, my mother's cousin, Miss Nancy Towle, of Hampton, N. H., a feminine evangelist, had encountered Smith in Ohio, and had reproved him publicly for his hypocrisy and wickedness—little surmising that his humbug would develop into a powerful Territory of the United States, and afterward a considerable State, now Utah, and not wholly under Mormon guidance.

The pistol of T. B. Eldridge did not give me as good service as the shawl. I carried it, contrary to my general rule not to go armed, except with a good stick, until I had passed through all the region supposed to be infested with Border Ruffians (the name, not undeserved, by which we knew the Missourian invaders of Kansas), and had never occasion to show even the butt of it. Finally, as I was driving on the homeward stretch one day, from Nebraska City, on the western bank of the Missouri River, to Council Bluffs, on the Iowa side, it occurred to me to try the effect of the weapon on the prairie chickens that were flying and alighting all about me on the wheat-growing fields of Iowa and the wild lands of the "Missouri Bottom." I stopped my driver there and got out of the light wagon he was driving to get a near shot at a covey of chickens in the roadway just behind us, where they had settled down after we had passed along. It was customary then to shoot them from a wagon anywhere on the open prairie, and we often had them for dinner or supper, amid the other uneatable food. I snapped every percussion cap of my six barrels at the birds without starting them from

the ground, but no charge went off. The powder
had fallen down from the nipple of the barrel, and
the bursting cap failed to ignite the powder in the
barrel itself. How I should have defended myself
in an actual fight with a Missourian I hardly know
—perhaps as General Jackson did, by thrusting his
hand in his coat-pocket and snapping the cover of
his snuff-box as he moved angrily toward his foe-
man—only, unluckily, I had not my grandfather's
snuff-box with me.

We reached Council Bluffs in the slow stage-
coach westward one August night as the red sun
was setting over the Missouri Bottom and the swift
river beyond it, where now stands the great city
of Omaha. In 1856 a single house marked the
spot, if I recollect aright. Council Bluffs was a
military station of the national army, and I found
there a good hotel, three or four miles from the
landing of the steamboat that was to carry me
down-stream to Nebraska City. A river boat was
tied up there, for an evening ball, after which it
would start in the night for St. Louis. I supped
well at the hotel, and then, under a bright moon, in
a huge stage-wagon, I found myself seated beside
a handsome, black-coated Kentuckian, wearing a
wide Byron collar and conspicuous shirt-cuffs. He
was going to the same steamer, in company with a
slender, fair-haired Lieutenant Foster of the army.
He was about my own age, and very conversable.
Soon he revealed himself as George Greathouse,
son of a county clerk in Kentucky—the county in
which both Henry Clay and Thomas Hart Benton

had found their wives, who were sisters. He knew the Benton family (Mr. Clay was dead), and in company with Randolph Benton, a son of the Senator from Missouri, had accompanied one of the expeditions of Colonel Frémont across the Rockies. But in 1856 he was opposed to Benton, who was then a candidate for Governor of Missouri, and he gave me some details of the election campaign, which was going on or had just closed. He said he was going out on the plains with his friend Foster, of the army, to shoot the buffalo, then very common in Nebraska and Kansas. Arrived at the steamboat landing, we found (as he had anticipated) that a ball was to begin at once, and after securing our staterooms for down the river, he prepared for taking part in it—having already, at the hotel, arrayed himself in funereal black for the festive occasion— the color and costume then deemed suitable for balls. He found a partner in a pretty girl in blue silk with a muslin waist, and danced with her several times. When I had disburdened myself of the heavy revolver in my stateroom, I joined him in the steamer's saloon, and between the dances we continued our conversation about Missouri and the Bentons and Frémont. The latter was then a candidate for the presidency, and I listened with interest to what he told me about a man I had never seen and whom he had known years before. Of course I did not disclose the capacity in which I was then traveling, and we avoided by mutual consent the topic of the Kansas troubles.

In the evening after the ball I left the steamer

at Nebraska City, bidding my Kentucky friend
farewell, and not expecting to see him again, as he
was to land some miles below and go out on the
plains. I found that I had not time to enter Kansas through Nebraska, as Colonel Higginson did
a few weeks later. I spent the Sunday in Nebraska City, saw the Free-State men there, including red-shirted riders from Kansas, and on Tuesday started by land up the river to Council Bluffs
on my return. We stopped at a small town, either
Sidney or Tabor, in Frémont County, Iowa, for
dinner, and waited there an hour or two until our
horse had eaten and digested his meal. As I was
strolling about the little tavern, after dinner,
whom should I come upon at the stable but my
Kentucky friend, with two or three horses, which
he was feeding. No longer in ballroom black, he
was dressed in the prairie costume of gray flannel
and boots, without a coat. I spoke to him and said,
"Why are you here, and not out on the prairie
shooting buffaloes?" He hung his head, and replied, "Down in Missouri they told me that the
abolitionists are making trouble in Kansas, and I
am going in with some of our men to put a stop
to it." I urged him not to do so, saying that he
had better keep out of harm's way, for " the dra-
goons of Uncle Sam will keep the peace there, and
you will not be needed." He said that he had promised to go in, and must keep his word. He did so,
joined an invading party, and was shot in a skirmish near Franklin, in the vicinity of Lawrence.
My friend Edmund Whitman, when I saw him

afterward in Massachusetts, where he spoke in October at some of the Kansas meetings for which I had made arrangements—one, I remember, was at Carlisle, near Concord—told me that he had seen Greathouse lying dead on the prairie between Lawrence and Franklin. He remembered the incident, which was not uncommon in Kansas that year, from the singularity of the man's name (Greathouse), which he had never heard before. There were many of those who fought on the pro-slavery side, no doubt, as agreeable and as reckless as my Kentucky comrade of a single night.

I have lately found a mass of my family letters of 1856-1861, which contain an account of my tour through Iowa and a part of Nebraska in August, 1856, and may be cited as contemporary evidence. They were written to assure my mother of my safety and health, but they fix certain dates beyond question, and connect my Kentucky friend Greathouse with the armed invasion from Missouri in September of that year.

WESTERN JOURNEY OF AUGUST, 1856

Nebraska City, Saturday Night, Aug. 16, 1856.
My dear Mother:

I write you this some 1600 miles from home, on the western bank of the Missouri River; yet, by the time you get it I may be myself in New England again. I reached here to-night on the steamboat *Admiral*, at 6 o'clock, from Council Bluffs,—having come across Iowa in a stage-coach from Mt. Pleasant, near Burlington, Iowa, in three days and a half. Council Bluffs is a town of 2000 people, in the extreme west of Iowa, about three miles from the Missouri River. I only stopped there a couple of hours; for I got in from the eastward about 7 P. M., and left for the boat about nine. I slept on board last night, but only for two or three hours, for there was a ball given on the boat, and I did not go to bed till 3 A. M. or after. I have slept an hour or two to-day, and expect to sleep my fill to-night. I have been riding day and night since Tuesday morning, and have not slept a great deal except in the coach; still I am perfectly well, and not very tired.

(*Sunday Morning, Aug.* 17.) After a sleep of nine hours, and a decent breakfast, I feel a good deal refreshed, and am ready to start again on my travels. I shall go from here either up the river to Council Bluffs again, and from there back across Iowa in a stage-coach, —or shall wait a day or two here, and go down the river to St. Louis. But I shall go no farther west at all events. I learn here that there has been no fighting in Nebraska, but that General Lane's men have got into Kansas.

This " city " has a population of 1200 or 1500, and is fast growing. Four years ago there were no buildings here except the block fort, and one or two buildings belonging to it, and the place was called " Fort Kearney." In ten years, probably, it will be a real city of 40,000, with railroads running through it; although there is now no railroad within 250 miles. It is a very busy place, and there is much speculation here, as there is at Council Bluffs, and all along the river on this Nebraska side. There are half a dozen " cities " between here and Omaha (opposite Council Bluffs)—in some of which there are but three or four houses; but land is selling there at great prices. This place is finely situated on the hilly western bank of the Missouri, and I should think is healthy.

The river is in full view from where I am, and is less than half a mile off. Did you ever read a description of the Missouri? It is the strangest river in the world. It is from 50 to 150 rods wide, I should think, and at present has an average depth of ten feet, perhaps, in the channel,—but the water is now quite low. The Missouri rises nearly 2000 miles above here, and flows for 700 miles more before entering the Mississippi. It is very swift, —running five or six miles an hour, and as muddy as it can be. It is yellow, for that reason, the color of coffee with milk in it, in consequence of the soil it washes along with it. Its course is constantly changing, and it is full of snags. The banks keep falling in, now on one side, now on the other,—making it insecure building near the water's edge, even where the banks are high enough; and on one side or the other (here on the Iowa side) there is a wide meadow (called a "bottom") which is sometimes flooded, varying in width from three to 20 miles, very fertile. On this bottom-land no towns can be built, so that on the Iowa side, from here to Council Bluffs, there can be no towns on the river, unless fortified by embankments, levees, etc.

There is great beauty in the banks of the river, and the stream itself; especially when seen by moonlight, as I first saw it, sweeping down so swiftly with its wide waters, it is a majestic sight. The country all around is now green and fertile, and must soon become thickly settled. The people here expect a railroad through from Burlington in course of five years,—I saw it building as I came through,—which will greatly benefit this city and will go on to make part of the great Pacific Railroad. I think it will be built through to here in two years, and I shall urge this on all Eastern capitalists as a most important object.

All through Iowa I rode amid beautiful rolling prairies, and saw a great deal of wood,—more than I expected. Governor J. W. Grimes, of Iowa, with whom I took tea at Burlington last Sunday evening, the 10th, told me there will always be wood enough in his State; that there is more there now than 25 years ago. The land is not so level as I thought,—not so level as Hampton and many parts of Hampton Falls,—and we crossed some hills steeper and longer than any about home. Iowa is the finest State I have yet seen for land—you never saw such Indian corn as they raise there. I saw a stalk on Friday which must have been 15 feet high,—perhaps 16 ; I could just reach the topmost ear on it without standing tiptoe, which means eight feet from the ground. They call our humble New England cornfields " bumblebee corn " ; for they say a bee can sit down at his ease and gather honey from its topmost flowers. I saw whole fields in the Missouri bottom where it was ten, twelve and fourteen feet high. Wheat had been cut; but I saw its immense stacks all along the road, for there are few barns in Iowa, except in a few of the southeast counties.

As I rode from Mount Pleasant to Council Bluffs I saw the sun rise from the eastern prairies and set behind the western ones; and finally I saw him set across the Missouri, and beyond the western plains and woods, where they hunt the buffalo. We passed many emigrant wagons, —the " prairie schooner,"—moving on by day and stationary at night, with a little fire beside them, where men and women were cooking their supper, as I have seen the Barrington gypsies doing at Hampton Falls. On Friday morning, the 15th, we came to a great camp of Mormons in Cass County,—some 300 women and children on their way to Utah, on foot or in ox-teams. They were from

England mostly,—poor, ignorant, and grossly deluded. I talked with several of them, and bought from their American leader a tract on " The Plurality of Wives." Large bodies of Mormons are before and behind these people; all moving to Utah, and most of them from Europe. One day earlier, as we were walking up a long hill, we killed a rattlesnake, no larger than our brown adders,—it was killed with the foot by one of us, without trouble. In the woodlands,—here called " timber,"— they grow larger; but on the prairie are always small.

I wrote to Sarah from the town of Winterset, the other day, and before that to Charles from Mt. Pleasant; but have heard nothing from New England since I left there, except through the New York newspapers for a few days; for I travel faster than the mails, usually. The latest paper I saw was the New York *Herald* at Burlington. Here they have no papers later than the St. Louis *Republican* and *Democrat* of the 6th,—but a boat is now looked for with two days' later dates. I shall look for letters at Mt. Pleasant or Chicago. I expect to be in Springfield by the 27th or 28th, and in Concord by the last of August or 1st of September. You will get this, I think, about the 30th. I have been well all the time, and have much enjoyed the trip. I have also done much business, and got many facts together. From Mt. Pleasant I have carried a revolver, lent me by Colonel T. B. Eldridge,—but in my valise; and I shall not wear it unless I go down the Missouri to St. Louis. This is a peaceful town, and I have seen no quarrels yet, anywhere.

I am always
Your affectionate son,
FRANK B. SANBORN.

Des Moines City, or Fort Des Moines, Aug. 22, 1856.
I got here at noon to-day, Friday, on my way home.
I left Nebraska City on Tuesday morning, the 19th,
waited a day at Sidney, just the Iowa side of the river,
—got to Council Bluffs by wagon at 10 P. M. on Wednesday,—left there yesterday at one o'clock in the morning, shall leave here at 3:30 A. M. to-morrow, Saturday.
I expect to get to Mt. Pleasant on Sunday, the 24th, and
to reach Chicago Tuesday morning, traveling all night.
I shall then reach Springfield Thursday afternoon, the
28th.   I am not very tired, and perfectly well.

Since I wrote, on the 17th, I have heard important news,
some of which you and Charles may hear before you get
this,—but some of it you will not hear.

I saw three of Martin Stowell's Worcester company of
emigrants on the 18th at Nebraska City; they told me of
the safe arrival of all Lane's men in Kansas.   They
founded three towns in Kansas as they went in,—one
five miles from the Nebraska line, called Plymouth, one
15 miles farther south,—Lexington,—and one as much
farther,—Concord.   Stowell's men are at Lexington, where
they have some 70 settlers.   It is a fine locality; the men
are well; they met no resistance, and are in good spirits.
An account of them has been sent to the New York
Tribune; another I send to the Boston *Telegraph;* so
you will soon see about this in the newspapers.   The success of the party was perfect.   But something has since
happened of which you have probably heard an exaggerated account.

As a portion of Lane's men (less than 100), were passing from Topeka to Lawrence on August 15,—they had
reached Topeka on the 11th,—they were fired on from
a block-house near Lecompton by pro-slavery men.   A
fight ensued.   Lane himself, who was behind, came up,

and as there was no other way of routing the pro-slavery men, the house was burned. None were killed, but three wounded on each side. These are the facts, as I had them from Lane's messenger, through another man,— and I also saw a letter from Lane. But in Missouri they report that Lecompton has been taken by Lane, and burned, the United States troops captured, and the prisoners released. Consequently, the Border Ruffians are sending in armed men to attack our men, and, if possible, to close up the route through Nebraska against emigrants. This they will fail to do; but there will no doubt be more serious fighting. Lane's men have acted so wisely and posted themselves so well, that I don't believe they can be driven out of their towns. I longed to go down into Kansas, but felt that I ought not. I spent two days at Nebraska City, because I could not get away. I do not think I shall be delayed any more; and you may confidently believe me at Springfield, when you get this letter on Friday, as you probably will.

[I did, in fact, carry the letter with me to Albany, N. Y., and there mailed it to Hampton Falls, N. H., after midnight, on the 28th,—adding in a postscript, " I shall be in Springfield at eleven this morning." This was Thursday and it did reach its destination on Friday the 29th.] This is a town of 3000 to 4000 people, on the Des Moines River. It is to be the capital of the State, and is a pleasant town. I shall have had enough of traveling before I get home, and shall be glad to get back to New England again.

Yours affectionately,
Frank B. Sanborn."

The attack and success of August 15 are correctly described in this letter. But when Atchison, in Missouri, August 17, was relating it, in order to incite his friends to invade Kansas again, as they did, he thus reported it:

" August 15, Brown, with 400 abolitionists, mostly Lane's men, mounted and armed, attacked Treadwell's Settlement in Douglas County, numbering about 30 men. They planted the old cannon ' Sacramento ' towards the colony, and surrounded them."

John Brown, Jr., one of the Lecompton prisoners, wrote from the prison camp to his father and brother Jason a more exact account, saying:

" I was in hearing of the attack on Colonel Titus this morning.   A messenger has just come in, stating that Titus and several others were taken prisoners; Titus wounded.   I saw the fire of Titus's house. . . . I should think that 200 shots have been fired within the past half-hour, within a mile of our camp.   Have just learned that some 80 of our Free State men have pitched in to a pro-slavery camp this side of Lecompton, which was commanded by a notorious pro-slavery scoundrel named Titus, —one of the Buford party from Alabama.   A dense volume of smoke is now rising in the vicinity of his house. The firing has ceased."

It was by the appeal of Atchison and Stringfellow on August 17, that my companion, the Kentuckian, Greathouse, was induced to join the invading force which Governor Geary sent back to Missouri about the middle of September, a month after this capture of Titus and his block-house. I parted from Greathouse at Nebraska City on

the 16th of August; he went farther down the
river and there met the news of the capture of Ti-
tus, and the other victories of the Free-State men.
I met him the second time at Tabor, or near there,
on the 20th, with his horses, and he no doubt joined
the army of invasion a few days later. At this time
Frederick and Jason Brown were the only sons of
Captain Brown who were with him in Kansas; for
Owen and his brother-in-law, Henry Thompson,
were in Tabor, wounded, and the younger sons,
Salmon and Oliver, were on their way back to
North Elba, where I saw Salmon the next summer.
Writing on August 19th, from his prison camp,
John Brown, Jr., said:

"Father returned to Kansas with the overland emigrants, leaving in Nebraska Henry Thompson, Owen, Salmon, Frederick and Oliver, much improved in health.
He was in the fight at Franklin, and also aided in routing
the gang on Washington Creek, as well as in the capture
of Titus and his crew. . . . He is an omnipresent
dread to the ruffians. I see by the Missouri papers that
they regard him as the most terrible foe they have to
encounter."

Writing from Tabor, August 27, Owen Brown
said:

"We hear lately that about 3000 Missourians have
crossed at St. Joe and other places, and have gone armed
into the Territory; that Governor Woodson has sent 400
mounted men on to the frontier [of Nebraska] to inter-
cept our volunteers, and prevent them from carrying in
provisions and ammunition, which are much needed now

in Kansas. . . . Nor have I heard from Henry, Salmon, William (Thompson) and Oliver, since they left this place (Tabor) to go home (to North Elba)."

My own errand in this journey was to inspect the emigrant route through Iowa, in order that it might be kept open for men, arms and ammunition during the autumn of 1856; and I was only to enter Kansas, if there was time for it, or urgent necessity. There was no time, for my school was to open early in September, and the news I got at Nebraska City was that our friends were successful. I believe I met Colonel Higginson at Worcester, August 29, before he went out to Kansas, to lead in a party of emigrants from Nebraska City early in September,—an adventure which he described at the time in letters to the New York *Tribune,* and more recently, with some inaccuracies, in his " Cheerful Yesterdays."

During a recent visit to me in Concord, Mr. W. E. Connelley, the best informed historian of Kansas and western Missouri,—the region in which he has lived for the past 30 years,—has informed me of a conversation lately held with the octogenarian, P. P. Elder (an early settler in Kansas from Maine), at one time Lieutenant-Governor, who informed him that in the early autumn of 1856 there was a definite agreement between Brown, Lane and Charles Robinson, then nominal Governor of the Territory, and Geary, at Lawrence, that they should all leave Kansas, and give Geary, the newly arrived Federal Governor, a

free hand in establishing peace between the war-
ring parties. His statement on this point was
questioned by Mr. Oswald Villard, who is prepar-
ing a new biography of Brown; but it agrees with
the recorded facts. All these Free-State leaders
did leave Kansas in September or early October,
1856; and in an address to the Kansas Historical
Society, January 18, 1881, Robinson said:

" On the 14th of September the Missouri army, 2800
strong, arrived at Lawrence, threatening its destruction.
. . . As these men were marching into the Territory,
I met Governor Geary at Lawrence, and had a full and
frank discussion of the situation. . . . John Brown
was present [in Lawrence]. I saw him constantly, as
neither of us had any connection with any company, and
could go as we pleased. . . . Governor Geary assured me that he . . . would guarantee the safety
of the town. . . . When the reconnoitering party
came in sight of Lawrence, I dispatched a messenger and
reminded the Governor of his pledge and the situation.
He at once sent the whole force of United States troops
with him to Lawrence, where they arrived in the night
and put an end to all anxiety. . . . Governor Geary
called to his aid several companies of *bona fide* residents
of the Territory, one of them commanded by Captain
Samuel Walker, and the war of extermination came to
an end. Geary was satisfied that the Free-State men
were largely in the majority, and was desirous that the
majority should rule; . . . he sent to the Governor
under the Topeka Constitution and desired an interview
at his office, . . . in the attic of the log cabin on
the bank of the river at Lecompton. At that interview
Governor Geary was ready to favor an admission under

the Topeka Constitution, and was ready to use his influence with the President and his party in Congress. It
was thought, if there could be a vacancy in the position
of Governor, that he or some other Democrat might be
elected to fill it. . . . Accordingly, the Topeka Governor resigned, and went to Washington, for the purpose of procuring admission into the Union." *

Robinson is careful not to give dates after September 16, when the Missouri army, dispersed by
Geary, began their retreat. But on September
22 Lane, from western Iowa, going eastward to
make speeches for Frémont, sent a letter to his
former fellow-soldier of the Mexican War, Doni-
phan, and did not return to Kansas for weeks and
months. About the middle of October, Robinson
was in Boston, making a speech, which I heard,
and on the 22d of October he made a speech for
Frémont in New York City. By December 1
Robinson was back in Kansas, to start the vanished
town of Quindaro, and it was not until December
25, 1856, that he sent a letter to his Lieutenant-
Governor, Roberts, resigning his nominal governorship. This was first published in the New York
Tribune of January 14, 1857.

During all the time from October 9 till the
summer of 1857, John Brown was out of Kansas,
and it is every way probable that he tacitly assented
to the arrangement with Geary, who had favored
his escape from arrest. Lane, who was not yet at
sharp variance with Robinson, may have given

*Proceedings of the Kansas Historical Society, Vols. 1 and 2.

Geary assurance of *his* absence, and was soon in Washington, laboring for the admission of Kansas as a State, under the Topeka Constitution. But the election of Buchanan as President, and the coming Dred Scott decision of the Supreme Court, intended to make negro slavery national and irremovable, cut short the intrigue, to which Geary may have been a party, and on the 4th of March, 1857, he resigned. I met him in Philadelphia soon after, loud in his denunciations of Buchanan and his policy.

All this time, from June to September, 1856, bodies of immigrants and individuals had been making their way into the Territory—some, but by no means all, through the agency of the Emigrant Aid Company, of Boston. This company had been very active in aiding immigrants and sending rifles during 1855 and 1856, but had suffered much by loss of its property from the Missouri raids. It left the work, in the later months of 1856 and the whole year 1857, largely to the National Kansas Committee and the Massachusetts State Committee, and to Gerrit Smith, who gave a thousand dollars a month during the active period of hostilities in 1856, and for some months longer. The State committee, of which I became secretary, used the funds of a Faneuil Hall committee, after the thorough organization of the State committee by the election of George L. Stearns as its chairman; having previously had its funds used in a masterly way by Dr. Howe, during the months of June and July. From about the first of August, 1856, Mr. Stearns

and his State committee became the working center
of aid to the Free-State men of Kansas, and were
heartily seconded by the Middlesex County Committee, of which I had been secretary since early
in June; by the Worcester County Committee, of
which Wentworth Higginson was an active member, and by the Hampden County Committee, of
which my brother-in-law, George Walker, was
chairman.

From Council Bluffs, on my stage-coach return
to Burlington, I took a new route part of the way,
and passed through Des Moines, which had been
designated as the capital of Iowa, and where the
State House was building. I had been sleeping
sweetly on the top of the coach, among the light
luggage, wrapped in Eldridge's shawl from the
heavy dews and the prairie breeze, always blowing,
when I awoke to find our vehicle trundling down
into the Des Moines valley, with the building-stone
for the new Capitol lying all about on the roadsides.
I have not been there since, in the fifty-two years
that intervene; but it is now a city of 80,000 people,
rich in manufactures; and in the State House which
I saw building, or in a more magnificent State Library since built, is a special " Alcott Room," devoted to the books, manuscripts, etc., of the Alcott
family, in honor of my contemporary, Louisa Alcott, who in that very year was watching the sick-
bed of her mother and sister " Beth," in Walpole,
N. H.—far enough from the fame which her family histories of " Little Women " were to bring her
a dozen years later.

I returned to Concord without further adventure, and took up my school-work; but along with it the continued business of raising money and holding meetings in aid of free Kansas. In December, 1856, putting my school in charge of the late Francis Abbot, then a student at Harvard College, for a few months, I took charge myself of the State Kansas Committee's office in Niles' Building, School Street, Boston—being secretary and general agent of the committee, of which my friend G. L. Stearns was chairman, and Dr. Howe, Dr. Samuel Cabot, Thomas Russell of Plymouth, afterward judge and railroad commissioner, and Minister to Venezuela, were active members, with Patrick Jackson, second of the name, and uncle of my intimate college friend, Charles Russell Lowell, as the treasurer. Out of this committee-work soon grew my intimacy with John Brown, of Kansas and Virginia.

Circumstances have made me, as testimony is measured in our courts of law, a competent and fairly credible witness as to the struggle to make Kansas a free State, and most of the men who took part in that struggle. I knew quite thoroughly, I think, the early history of Kansas, both as unorganized and disorganized Territory and as a State in the Union. I became interested in that sparsely settled Territory, not as a landholder or settler, but as a friend of free institutions, early in 1855, when I was of full age and able to understand facts and draw inferences—so far as a course of instruction at Harvard College could enable me. I kept up

my acquaintance with events and persons there
through the whole disturbed period, from 1855 to
1862, by correspondence, travel, and careful reading of the conflicting evidence furnished by newspapers, Presidents' messages, and printed books
and speeches. I never allowed my opinions to be
biased by buying lands there, or running for office.
I expended a year's time, first and last, and what
was for me a good deal of money, to make Kansas
a free State, and have three times visited it and
traveled through portions of it, to see what had
been the upshot of our early efforts. I have never
been hired, as several of the would-be historians
and chroniclers of Kansas were, to write up any
man's merits or write down any man's faults. I
am therefore puzzled sometimes to know why I
should be attacked and traduced by men whose
cause I espoused when the whole force of the national government was against them, and with
whom I had no quarrel until they picked one themselves with me. I am a member of the Kansas Historical Society, which has collected the largest mass
in the world of the documents illustrating the early
history of the State; have spent days examining
this collection, and been in friendly correspondence
with its secretaries from the beginning.

I can therefore speak from actual knowledge
with regard to most of the persons active in the
settlement of the disputed questions in Kansas, and,
I think, have always been able to judge with reasonable impartiality of their conduct and motives.
I did not know the weak but good-natured Presi-

dent, Franklin Pierce, during his term of office, but I made his acquaintance later, and think I understand the lamentable inconsistencies in his character. I met Governor Geary on his return from his useful but thankless task of undoing the mischief occasioned by the misconduct of President Pierce, under the stronger will of Jefferson Davis, his Secretary of War; and I understood what qualities had aided and what hindered his work in Kansas. I spent an afternoon with A. H. Reeder, the first Territorial Governor of Kansas, at his home in Easton, Pa., and could measure his qualities, such as they were; and I met, first and last, nearly all the active persons who aided in the desired result. They had various gifts, and by no means all the same spirit; but among them all none was so truly remarkable as John Brown. Other men might have been spared; he was indispensable. We did not all see this at the time; some persons dispute it now; but the fact remains, and will only become more evident as time passes, and gradually sets the deeds of all men who are not entirely forgotten in their proper perspective.

I was sitting in my small office in School Street early in January, 1857, when Brown entered, and handed me a letter of introduction from my brother Walker of Springfield. He had known Brown as a neighbor and borrower of bank loans while carrying on a large business in Springfield as a wool-dealer; indeed, George Walker was, I believe, the legal counsel of one of the banks which Brown used in his loans and payments. Hardly any two men were more unlike by nature and training, except that both had honest and kindly hearts. George was a scholarly and carefully trained man, who had cultivated the graces and amenities of life and moved in a circle of affectionate politeness, at first in New Hampshire, where he was born in 1824, and afterward at Boston and Springfield, where he married the only daughter of a wealthy family, and lived in ease and moderate luxury, surrounded by his books, his children, his friends and his guests. He had political opinions, but not strong ones; had inherited from his father and his great-uncle, Judge Smith, of New Hampshire, Webster's friend, the old-fashioned sentiments of the Federalists and their grandchildren, the Whigs. He was humane, sensible, considerate; detested negro slavery, but saw no way to rid the nation of it; studied English history, literature and finance, and might well have been a professor of law or political economy at Dartmouth, Yale, or Harvard, all colleges which he knew as a student there.

John Brown, though born in New England, and strongly marked with the New England seriousness of mood, had spent most of his half-century in new and wild regions, intimate with nature, and directing other men rather than guided or trained by them. He was profound in his thinking, and had formed his opinions rather by observation than by reading, though well versed in a few books, chief among which was the Bible. He was, in truth, a Calvinistic Puritan, born a century or two after the fashion had changed; but as ready as those of

JOHN BROWN, 1857
From a Boston Photograph

Bradford's or Cromwell's time had been to engage in any work of the Lord to which he felt himself called. He saw with unusual clearness the mischievous relation to republican institutions of negro slavery, and made up his fixed mind that it must be abolished; not merely, or even mostly, for the relief of the slaves, but for the restoration of the Republic to its original ideal—freedom under law for all, white, black, yellow or red. He regarded the Indian and the negro simply as men; and though he did not expect of them what he expected of his own race and faith, he believed that all their rights should be respected. He had seen the country coming more and more into the belief that slavery was a permanent institution—not as Jefferson and Washington had looked on it, something that must gradually yield to the spirit of freedom embodied in the American ideal. He had formed various plans for attacking slavery where it was apparently strongest, but really weakest—in the midst of the large plantations. The effort to give the evil institution renewed vitality by annexing new territory for colonization by slaveholders, alarmed him in the Mexican War, and aroused him to decisive action when Kansas was opened by the slave-masters, then in control of the national government, to the blighting introduction and spread of negro slavery. He saw the proper remedy for this mischief—the colonization of the Territory by free laborers—as soon as any man had seen it; and his four sons were among the early settlers in Kansas. He had joined them there, in October, 1855, with arms and sup-

plies, intended for the defense of them and of other
pioneers against the invaders from the South.

It so happened that the whole North had been
shocked by the repeal of the Missouri Compromise
of 1820, under pressure from the President and his
cabinet; and the Whig party was startled in a
greater degree than its Democratic or Native American opponents. Mr. Walker had been an active
Whig, and was overtaken, along with his party in
Massachusetts, by the " Know-Nothing" flood in
1854, after the marriage and death of his sister,
which brought me into close relations with him.
From that time he was ready, like so many others
of the young Whigs, to unite with any citizens resolved against the further extension of slavery. He
had joined the newly formed Republican party in
1856, and was enthusiastic for the election of Frémont, as I was. He knew Brown's sterling integrity of old, and had followed his career in Kansas
more closely than I had. Hence his readiness to
promote Brown's wishes in the winter of 1856-57;
to forward which the Kansas fighter had come to
Boston. And with my introduction to Brown that
winter day, there began an episode in my life which
had unexpected and most important results.

CHAPTER III

Kansas and Virginia

MUCH of my youthful life had been put behind me at the beginning of this friendship with John Brown, and it had been marked by singular and providential incidents; so that I was prepared for the faith which I soon learned that Brown entertained in a Power which directs or leads men beyond their own expectations, hopes or wishes. Like others who have reached seven-and-seventy years (or much fewer than that), I have often noticed in looking back how one marked event in early life leads to another marked event, and that to a third, and so on; as if by a chain of sequences arranged beforehand upon a scheme of life. It is this, no doubt, which has led so many men to view their careers as something foreordained—a map shown of their destinies, which pointed out the way they were to go, not compelling them to a given course, but indicating the line of least resistance. It was through the fact that my fathers had been parishioners of Parson Abbot, and the acquaintance had been kept up between the families, that I became the lover of Ariana Walker. It was she who determined my college education; it was our mutual interest for the oppressed that made me active in the cause of social

and political freedom; and it was her brother
George, a year or two after her death, who sent
John Brown of Kansas to me with a letter of
introduction, late in the year 1856. Six years later
it was this same brother-in-law, then in the State
government of Massachusetts (when the John
Brown episode had been closed by the emancipation
proclamation of Abraham Lincoln, and the victory
at Gettysburg), who suggested to me an appointment on the newly created Board of State Charities, in 1863, which has largely shaped the course
of my public life for nearly half a century. From
another point of view, my college career brought
me into the circle of the Concord Transcendental-
ists, and determined that small focus of plain living
and high thinking as my place of abode for more
than half a century—save for a few years that I
resided near my brother-in-law in Springfield.
And it was the acquaintance formed with his circle
at Springfield, from 1853 to 1865, which led to my
selection by his intimate friend, Samuel Bowles,
as one of the editors of the *Springfield Republican,*
—then and since one of the most influential journals in the United States; whose staff I joined in
1856, as a correspondent, and of which I became
a resident editor in 1868, and until 1872.

I cannot believe, therefore, that our human
lives are subject to blind chance, or fortuitously
directed by accident. Too many events in my own
career and those of my associates, have shown me
a more intelligent directing power, aside from the
individual human will; what it is, in direct activity,

I have not too curiously inquired. But I have followed its intimations when they were clearly revealed, and thus have found my little bark steered by a hand wiser than my own.

This faith is one aspect of that philosophy to which mere accident may have given, in America, the name of "Transcendental," and of which my long-time friends, Alcott and Emerson, were the best representatives—unless it might be some simple-hearted Quakeress, illumined by the Inner Light. John Brown, that descendant of *Mayflower* Pilgrims, held this faith also, and it led him into those dark, heroic ways whose issue was the forcible destruction of negro slavery, and his own immortality of fame, as one of the two grand martyrs of that cause—Abraham Lincoln being the other. I have met many men and women of eminent character, and of various genius and talents, among whom Brown stands by himself—an occasion for dispute and blame as well as for praise and song. I belong now to a small and fast-dwindling band of men and women who, fifty, sixty and seventy years ago resolved that other persons ought to be as free as ourselves. Many of this band made sacrifices for the cause of freedom—the freedom of others, not their own. Some sacrificed their fortunes and their lives. One man, rising above the rest by a whole head, gave his life, his small fortune, his children, his reputation—all that was naturally dear to him—under conditions which have kept him in memory, while other victims are forgotten or but dimly remembered. John Brown fastened the gaze of the whole world upon his acts and his fate; the speeding years have not lessened the interest of mankind in his life and death; and each succeeding generation inquires what sort of man he truly was. The time is coming—and has already arrived in some regions—when Brown will be regarded as a mythical personage, incarnating some truth or some desire dear to the human race, but not a flesh-and-blood man at all. His career had elements of romance and improbability, such as make us doubt the actual existence of legendary heroes, like Hercules, Samson, Arthur, Roland and the Spanish Cid. But he was a very real and actual person—only a peculiar and remarkable one, like Joan of Arc—one of those who appear from time to time, to verify the saying, "Man alone can perform the impossible." What more impossible than that a village-girl of France should lead the king's armies to victory?—unless it were that a sheep-farmer and wool-merchant of Ohio should foreshow and rehearse the forcible emancipation of four millions of American slaves.

Brown knew the inward cancer that was destroying our Republic; he pointed to the knife and the cautery that must extirpate it; he even had the force and nerve to make the first incision. Lord Rosebery, speaking of certain national junctures, says, "What is then wanted is not treasures, nor fleets, nor legions, but a *man*—the man of the moment, the man of destiny. In such there is (besides their talents) their spirit, their character—that magnetic fluid which enables them to influence vast

bodies of their fellow-men; and makes them a
binding and stimulating power outside the circle
of their own fascination." This character Brown
had; it grew out of his courage, his self-sacrifice
and his implicit faith in God. These are traits that
cannot long be simulated, nor is it easy to disguise
self-seeking in a mask of generosity. The less
courage, the more self-love men have, the more
quick are they to recognize their opposites.

It has been asked if from the first the greatness
of Brown's nature and mission was perceived. Of
course they were not seen by all; but there is a di-
vining quality in youth and in genius which lets
them behold in simple men more than the callous
veteran may discern. From my first meeting with
him, as from his first interviews with Thoreau and
Emerson, to whom I introduced Brown, it was clear
to them as to me that he was no common man; his
face, his walk, his whole bearing proclaimed it.
Like Cromwell, whom in certain rare qualities he
much resembled, he had " cleared his mind of
cant "; the hollow formulas of scholars, priests and
politicians had little force with Brown. He had a
purpose, knew what it was, and meant to achieve
it. Who may say that he did not? The emancipation of our slaves could not be the work of any
one man, or of a million men; it was finally wrought
by Lincoln with a stroke of his pen; but even then
it cost thousands of lives and the patient work of
years to confirm what Lincoln had written. John
Brown convinced the leaders of opinion on both
sides that slavery must die or the nation could not

live; and that was the first long step towards our emancipation.

I first met Brown, a little more than fifty years ago, when he was not yet 57 years old; my acquaintance with him continued hardly three years; yet I seem to have known him better, and to have seen him oftener than those who have journeyed beside me in life's path for sixty years. My actual intercourse with him hardly exceeded a month; my correspondence was some two and a half years (from February, 1857, to September, 1859), and that infrequent; yet the momentous events in which he had a share give to that brief intercourse the seeming duration of a lifetime. Nay, Thoreau was literally no less than figuratively right, when he ascribed to Brown a practical immortality. "Of all the men who were said to be my contemporaries, it seems to me that John Brown is the only one who has not died. I meet him at every turn. He is more alive than ever he was."

He came to me, as mentioned, with a note of introduction from George Walker—both of us being Kansas committee-men, working to maintain the freedom of that Territory,—and Brown had been one of the fighting men there in the summer of 1856, just before. His theory required fighting in Kansas; it was the only sure way to keep that region free from the curse of slavery. His mission now was to levy war on it, and for that to raise and equip a company of a hundred well-armed men who should resist aggression in Kansas, or occasionally carry the war into Missouri.

Behind that purpose, but not yet disclosed, was his intention to use the men thus put into the field for incursions into Virginia or other slave States. Our State Kansas Committee, of which I was secretary, had a stock of arms that Brown wished to use for this company, and these we voted to him. We did this in recognition of his past services in Kansas, which nobody of our way of thinking then disputed. His whole conduct in the Territory was not fully known to us; but it was fairly well understood in Kansas. He had reached Kansas in October, 1855, traveling slowly with his son-in-law, Henry Thompson, of North Elba, N. Y., through Illinois, Iowa and slave-holding Missouri. But his first introduction to the armed defenders of freedom at Lawrence in December, was thus described by G. W. Brown, in his *Herald of Freedom,* December 15, 1855:

"About noon [on Friday, December 7] Mr. JOHN BROWN, an aged gentleman from Essex County, N. Y., who has been a resident of the Territory for several months, arrived with four of his sons—leaving several others at home sick—bringing a quantity of arms with him, which were placed in his hands by eastern friends for the defense of the cause of freedom. Having more than he could well use to advantage, a portion of them were placed in the hands of those who were more destitute. A company was organized and the command given to Mr. B. for the zeal he had exhibited in the cause of freedom both before and since his arrival in the Territory."

This was in the midst of the first siege of Lawrence, then the leading Free State town in Kansas, in the so-called "Wakarusa War." There was more threatening than fighting; but in it Brown received his title of captain, given him as commander of the company in which his sons served. His own account of the affair, in a letter to his family in the Adirondac forest, written Sunday, December 16, from his brother-in-law's log cabin, near Osawatomie, is as follows, abbreviated:

" These reports [of murder and invasion from Missouri] appeared to be well authenticated, and I left this for the place where the boys are settled, at evening, intending to go to Lawrence to learn the facts the next day. John [his son] was, however, started on horseback; but before he had gone many rods, word came that our help was immediately wanted. We then set about providing a little corn-bread and meat, blankets, and cooking utensils, running bullets and loading our guns, pistols, etc. The five set off in the afternoon, and after a short rest in the night (which was quite dark), continued our march until after daylight next morning, when we got our breakfast, started again, and reached Lawrence in the forenoon, all of us more or less lamed by our tramp. On reaching the place we found that negotiations had commenced between Governor Shannon and the principal leaders of the Free-State men, they having a force of some five hundred men at that time. These were busy, night and day, fortifying the town with embankments and circular earthworks, up to the time of the treaty with the Governor, as an attack was constantly looked for, notwithstanding the negotiations then pending. This state of things continued from Friday until Sunday evening.

" After frequently calling on the leaders of the Free-State men to come and have an interview with him, by Governor Shannon, and after as often getting for an answer that if he had any business to transact with any one in Lawrence, to come and attend to it, he signified his wish to come into the town, and an escort was sent to the invaders' camp to conduct him in. When there, the leading Free-State men, finding out his weakness, frailty, and consciousness of the awkward circumstances into which he had really got himself, took advantage of his cowardice and folly, and by means of that and the free use of whiskey and some trickery succeeded in getting a written arrangement with him much to their own liking. He stipulated with them to order the pro-slavery men of Kansas home, and to proclaim to the Missouri invaders that they must quit the Territory without delay, and also to give up General Pomeroy (a prisoner in their camp)— which was all done; he also recognizing the volunteers as the militia of Kansas, and empowering their officers to call them out whenever in their discretion the safety of Lawrence or other portions of the Territory might require it to be done.

" One little circumstance, connected with our own number, showing a little of the true character of these invaders: On our way, about three miles from Lawrence, we had to pass a bridge (with our arms and ammunition) of which the invaders held possession; but as the five of us had each a gun, with two large revolvers in a belt exposed to view, with a third in his pocket, and as we moved directly on to the bridge without making any halt, they, for some reason, suffered us to pass without interruption, notwithstanding there were some fifteen to twenty-five (as variously reported) stationed in a log-house at one end of the bridge. We could not count them. A boy on our approach ran and gave them notice. Five others of our company, well armed, who followed some miles behind, met with equally civil treatment the same day. After we left to go to Lawrence, until we returned when disbanded, I did not see the least sign of cowardice or want of self-possession exhibited by any volunteer of the eleven companies who constituted the Free-State force; and I never expect again to see an equal number of such well-behaved, cool, determined men. . . . We all returned safe and well, with the exception of hard colds."

From that December day until he left Kansas ten months later, Brown was the most active and trusted hero of Kansas. Other men played their parts well, but Brown's was the name that made the deepest impression on friends and foes. His battles were skirmishes, but they had the twofold effect of alarming the slavery propaganda at Washington, and retaining on their farms the harassed and plundered citizens, until the aid and the weapons that our committees sent them put them in a good posture of defense. While I was traversing Iowa in the interest of the emigration from east of the Mississippi, Governor Geary, a Pennsylvania Democrat (who had been appointed to succeed the incompetent Shannon, and directed to " stop the fighting in Kansas " in the interest of Buchanan, the successful presidential candidate of that year), was proceeding up the Missouri River, to take command in the Territory, and do that very thing. So long as Missouri and

South Carolina were invading Kansas, and so long as Brown and Walker, Abbott, Shore, Montgomery, Lane, and other fighting leaders were in the field against them, the vote of Pennsylvania in the close contest for President was doubtful. Had it refused its vote to Buchanan, Frémont would have been elected, and the Civil War would have begun four years earlier than it did under Abraham Lincoln. Geary, in fact, sided with the Free State men, released the imprisoned Northern men, and allowed Brown to leave Kansas without being arrested for acts that could have been punishable under the wicked slave code of the Territory, imposed by voters from Missouri. For this conduct, after the election of Buchanan was made certain, and Geary's honest services were no longer required, he was removed by President Pierce, to whom he had written the truth about Kansas affairs. I saw him in Philadelphia in 1857, and he confirmed to me in conversation what he had written to General Pierce the winter before. Some of his words may be quoted: (Dec. 22, 1856.)

" I could not have credited it unless I had seen it with my own eyes, and had the most conclusive evidence of the fact—that public officers would have lent themselves to carry out schemes which at once set at naught every principle of right and justice upon which the equality and existence of our government is founded. You know that there is no man in the Union that more heartily despises the abolitionists than I do, or more clearly perceives the pernicious tendency of their doctrines; and on this question I trust I am an impartial judge. The persecutions of the Free-State men here were not exceeded by those of the early Christians. . . . The men holding official position have never given you that impartial information . . . which your high position so imperatively demanded. . . . I am satisfied that there was a settled determination in *high quarters*, to make this a Slave State *at all hazards;* that policy was communicated here, to agents, and most of the public officers sent here were secured for its success. The consequence was that when Northern emigrants came here at an early day— *even before* the Emigrant Aid Societies began to excite public attention—certain persons along the borders of Missouri began to challenge unexceptionable settlers. Finding many not for a slave State, they were subjected to various indignities, and told that this soil did not belong to such as them, and that they *must settle in Nebraska*. These immigrants, *highly conservative* in their character, excited by this unjust treatment, wrote back to their friends in the North; and thus by a little indiscretion on the part of over-zealous persons in Missouri, a spark was ignited which nearly set the whole country in a flame. This virulent spirit of dogged determination, to *force* slavery into this Territory, has overshot its mark, and raised a storm. . . . Lecompte, Donaldson, Clarke, Woodson, Calhoun, and Isaacs were prominent actors in this fearful tragedy, and willing tools to carry out this wicked policy. They have therefore destroyed their public usefulness."

While Governor Geary was thus truthfully and loyally describing to his official superior the proslavery conspiracy, Charles Robinson had given to John Brown this testimonial, and it was on its way to me, with the indorsements of Governor Chase of Ohio (afterward Chief Justice) and of Gerrit Smith. The Free State Governor of Kansas wrote to Brown (September 14, 1856):

"Your course, so far as I have been informed, has been such as to merit the highest praise from every patriot. . . . History will give your name a proud place on her pages, and posterity will pay homage to your heroism in the cause of God and humanity."

In his letters of 1884-1885, after deserting his party, Robinson struggled to show that this letter was a forgery. Before showing it to me, as Brown did early in January, 1857, he had shown it to Governor Chase of Ohio, who wrote (and I saw the note), dating December 20, 1856:

"I have also seen a letter from Governor Charles Robinson, whose handwriting I recognize, speaking of Captain Brown and his services to the cause of the Free-State men in Kansas in terms of the warmest commendation."

Brown showed this note and Robinson's longer letter (December 30, 1856) to Gerrit Smith, who then wrote:

"You did not need to show me letters from Governor Chase and Governor Robinson to let me know who and what you are. I have known you many years, and have highly esteemed you as long as I have known you."

I had met Charles Robinson in Boston in October, 1856, and had received letters from him for

our committee, so that I could also recognize the
handwriting when Brown showed me the two letters of Robinson in January, 1857. At the time
they were written Robinson had reason to know, as
I had not, that Brown had directed the Pottawatomie executions of May 24, 1856, immediately
after the sack of Lawrence by Atchison of Missouri and his followers. I shall speak of that matter later; but here I may quote what Colonel Sam
Walker, one of Brown's constant friends in Kansas, said to me in 1882, detailing a conversation he
had with Brown early in August, 1856, as they
were on an expedition to escort General Lane back
into Kansas:

"As we rode along together, Brown was in a sort of
study; and I said to him, ' Captain Brown, I wouldn't
have your thoughts for anything in the world.' Brown
said, ' I suppose you are thinking about the Pottawatomie
affair.' Said I, ' Yes.' Then he stopped and looked at
me, and said, ' Captain Walker, I saw that whole thing,
but I did not strike a blow. I take the responsibility of
it; but there were men who advised doing it, and afterward failed to justify it, . . .' [I believed him] for
Brown would never tell me what was not true, and would
not deny to me anything he had really done."

This conversation was about August 9. I published the substance of it in the Boston *Transcript*
in December, 1884—having got Walker's permission in 1882 to make it public. Being appealed to
by Robinson or Mr. Lawrence to contradict it,
Walker wrote to Robinson in a letter of December 16, 1884, from Lawrence:

+ one alive with twenty, Buck shot & Bullet holes in him, after the two murdered men had lain on the ground to be worked at by the flies for some 18 Hours. One of these young men was my own Son.

about the head

& I n Mr Parker who I will know, all bruised & with his throat partly cut; after being dragged sick from the House of Ottawa Jones, & thrown over the bank of the Ottawa Creek for dead: about the first of Sept

I u the five sick & wounded Sons, two Sons in Law were obliged to lie on the ground without shelter for a considerable time; our Books, & clothes worn out, destitute of money, & at times almost in a state of starvation; & dependant on the Charities of the Christian Indians & have before named, & his Wife.

FROM JOHN BROWN'S NOTES FOR A SPEECH

for being suspected of favouring the Free State Men

He is known as Ottawa Jones, or John Jones.

In Add Cont

Free State called Stanton

I visited a beautiful little town on the North side of the Orange or Meridezine as sometimes called; from which every inhabitant had fled for fear of their lives after having built a strong Block house or wooden fort at a heavy expense for their protection. Many of them had left their effects liable to be destroyed or carried off; not being able to remove them. This was a most gloomy scene & like a visit to a vast Sepulchre.

Deserted houses & cornfields were to be found in almost every direction South from the Kanzas river. By a body 400 Ruffians Aug 30th & of Franklin &c

I saw the burning of (Osawatomie ...

" Mr. Sanborn's article in the Boston *Transcript* is in
the main correct, except that Lane and you advised me
to go down to the Pottawatomie and kill those men. . . .
What I said was that Brown told me that you and Lane
advised him to strike a blow, and now when he had done
it you would not sustain him. I told him [Brown] such
a plan had been proposed to me, but there was no place
or party mentioned, but you was not one of the gentlemen that talked to me about it, and I do not wish to say
who they were."

It is quite possible that Lane was one of them,
for he was often wild in his talk.

A little before this conversation with Captain
Walker, John Brown had been seen by a Free State
settler in northern Kansas, Samuel Reader, living
near Pony Creek, and we have from his journal of
the period, revised some time afterward, a striking
picture of the Kansas hero on two occasions—Sunday, August 3, 1856, and again Thursday, August
7; the first time in Kansas, the second in Nebraska,
near the border-line. As he was out with his gun
on the first occasion, looking for game, he met two
men traveling northward with a covered wagon
drawn by a yoke of oxen. They proved to be John
Brown, with his son Frederick, or possibly his
youngest son, Oliver, but were then unknown to
Reader, who says:

" One was a young man, somewhat above the ordinary
height; the other, quite old. Both were walking, and
both were dusty, and travel-stained. The team was
stopped, and the old man inquired of me: ' Do you be-

long to a Free-State party, in camp near by?' I replied
that I did. 'Where is your camp?' I pointed in its direction, and was about to continue on my way, when he
detained me. 'Your coming has caused a good deal of
excitement among the Pro-Slavery men living on the
road. They didn't mind talking with us about it, as we
are surveyors.' He motioned with his hand toward the
wagon. I looked, and noticed for the first time a surveyor's chain hanging partly over the front end-board
of the wagon. Just behind was a compass and tripod,
standing up under the wagon cover. It struck me that
he might possibly be Pro-Slavery himself, so I answered
his direct questions, but ventured to make no remarks
myself. I had been cautioned to be very careful what
I said to men living along our line of march. The ox-
team naturally led me to suppose that these men were
settlers near by. . . . 'Where do you live?' he
asked. 'Indianola.' 'O yes! I know. It is a hard place,
and has got a very bad reputation. I have heard of it.'
'Have you ever been in a fight?' he next inquired. 'No.'
'Well,' he continued, 'you may possibly see some fighting, soon. If you ever *do* get in a battle, always remember to aim *low*. You will be apt to overshoot at first.'
Perhaps I smiled a little, for he added: 'Maybe you
think me a little free in offering advice; but I am somewhat older than you, and that ought to be taken in
account.' He said this gravely and pleasantly. The
younger man, behind him, was looking at me, with a broad
grin on his face, had not a word to say, but seemed
vastly amused at something. We separated. They
forded the [Pony] creek, and went in the direction of
[our] camp."

Reader presently met one of his party who told
him that the old man (Brown was fifty-six the 8th

of May before) was John Brown, at which Reader was delighted, because, he says, " even at that early date Brown was a very noted man, and was trusted and esteemed by all who held anti-slavery views." The same afternoon Reader's party broke camp and moved northward in a marching column, going to meet and escort some incoming Free State immigrants. Soon he had a chance to see Brown again, for he says:

" We had been on the road perhaps an hour or more, when some one in front shouted, ' There he is! ' Sure enough, it was Brown. Just ahead of us we saw the dingy old wagon-cover, and the two men, and the oxen, plodding slowly onward. As we passed the old man, on either side of the road, we rent the air with cheers. If John Brown ever delighted in the praises of men, his pleasure must have been gratified, as he walked along, enveloped in our shouting column. But I fear he looked upon such things as vainglorious, for if he responded by word or act I failed to see or hear it. I looked at him closely. He was rather tall, and lean, with a tanned, weather-beaten aspect, like a rough, hard-working old farmer. He appeared to be unarmed. His face was shaven, and he wore a cotton shirt, partly covered by a vest. His hat was well worn, and his general appearance, dilapidated, dusty, and soiled. He turned from his ox team and glanced at our party from time to time as we were passing him. At the top of the next ridge I glanced backward, and looked again at the homely, humble figure, following in our wake at a snail's pace."

Once more, on August 7, Reader saw Brown; this time mounted, and with the air of a comman-

der. The company was in Nebraska; the immigrants had been met, and were to cross the line into
Kansas. Reader goes on:

"We were about ready to start, when Col. Dickey
came over to us and read a paper of instructions from his
superiors. There it was in black and white, that armed
men should not escort the train when it crossed the line
into Kansas. Some heated discussion followed. Dickey
urged us to put our arms in the wagons, and as soon as
we were across the line we could take them back again.
Other men joined the Colonel, and expostulated with our
obdurate commander. [This was A. D. Stevens,* who
was with Brown at Harper's Ferry]. Captain Whipple
was standing a few feet in front of our line, and not three
paces from where I stood. A horseman rode up in front
of him. I looked up. It was Old Osawatomie Brown.
He addressed himself earnestly to Whipple.

"'Do as they wish. This train is to enter Kansas as
a peaceable emigrant train. It will never do to have it
escorted by armed men. As soon as we are across the
line, there will be no objection to your retaking your
arms. Let us all stay together. Your services may be
needed.'

"There was more to the same effect. Capt. Whipple
said but little in reply. He was striking the ground at
his feet with the point of his sword, during most of the
conversation. He looked obstinate, and sullen—something like a big school-boy when taken to task by his
teacher.

"'Perhaps,' added Brown, 'you don't know me; you
don't know who I am?'

"'Yes I do,' exclaimed Whipple; 'I know who you

* He then called himself Whipple.

are, well enough; but all the same, we are not going to
part with our arms. We came armed, and we're going
back armed.'

" I was somewhat surprised to learn by this conversation that Brown and Whipple were strangers to each
other. Brown saw that further entreaty would be use-
less. He turned, and rode away. It was the last time
I ever saw him."

After this scene, which proves the charge false
that Brown was always eager to attack the United
States troops in Kansas—which he never wished to
do—he returned to the scene of guerrilla warfare
near Lawrence, and remained there and near Osawatomie, where one of his most famous fights occurred, late in August, until he left the Territory
in October. Though urged to arrest him by the
pro-slavery party, Governor Geary had no more
wish to bring him to trial than President Lincoln
had, nine years after, to arrest Jefferson Davis,
after the capture of Richmond. Colonel Walker
in 1882 told me this anecdote of September, 1856,
to illustrate the perplexed situation under Governor Geary. He had made Walker, though the captain of a Free State band of eighty men, his United
States marshal, to serve processes and make arrests.
One morning, after one of Brown's exploits which
had made much noise, Geary sent a note to Walker,
as he was drilling his men out on the field, telling
him to get word to Brown that a warrant was out
against him, which *must* be served, and that Brown
must get away. Walker saw a man looking on
whom he had before seen in Brown's camp; he took

him one side, showed him Geary's note, and told
him to find and warn Brown, who was then on the
Wakarusa, some ten miles from Lawrence. Not
long after came an orderly from Governor Geary
with a warrant against Brown, which Walker (the
deputy marshal) must serve with his *posse*. "Take
him, dead or alive [was the order]; and for this I
shall hold you, Captain Walker, personally responsible." He took the warrant and made search for
Brown, who, of course, was not to be found.
Walker soon learned that the man he had sent to
warn Brown was James Montgomery, afterward a
fighter in Kansas and a colonel of colored soldiers
in the Civil War.

About this time General Lane was at Nebraska
City, where I had been three weeks earlier, and
Wentworth Higginson met him there—"a thin
man of middle age, in a gray woolen shirt, with
keen eyes, smooth tongue, and a suggestion of
courteous and even fascinating manners." Lane
was then retreating from Kansas in deference to
the orders of Geary, the new Governor, but delayed two days at Nebraska City, and made a
speech, of which Higginson says:

"I have seldom heard eloquence more thrilling, more
tactful, better adjusted to the occasion. Ralph Waldo
Emerson, I remember, was much impressed by a report
of this speech as sent by me to some Boston newspaper."

Lane was on his way East to take part in the
speaking campaign for Frémont, as he afterward
did for the election and re-election of Abraham

LOG-CABIN OF REV. S. L. ADAIR,
A Refuge of John Brown, Osawatomie, 1855-1858.

MR. ADAIR IN HIS CABIN

Lincoln. Brown came eastward much more slowly, only reaching Tabor, in Iowa, October 10, 1856. The next day he wrote to his family at North Elba, where I visited them for the first time the next August, the following letter:

"TABOR, IOWA, 11th Oct., 1856.

"*Dear Wife and Children, every one:*

"I am, through infinite grace, once more in a Free State; and on my way to make you a visit. I left Kansas a day or two since, by a wagon in which I had a bed; as I was so unwell that I had to lie down. I first had the dysentery, and then chill fever. Am now rapidly improving. Wealthy and Ellen [wives of John Brown, Jr., and Jason] with their little boys started for home by way of the River about ten days since. John, Jason and Owen all came out with me. John and Jason have gone on toward Chicago with a horse; but expect to meet me next week, on the Railroad on the East line of the State [Iowa]. I expect to go by stage. Owen thinks of wintering here.

"Mr. Adair and family were all middling well, two weeks ago. Mr. Day and family have been sick, but were better. When we left there seemed to be a little calm for the present in Kansas; cannot say how long it will last. You need not be anxious about me, if I am some time on the road, as I have to stop at several places. I go some out of my way, having left partly on business, expecting to return if the troubles continue in Kansas and my health will admit. Now that I am where I can write you, I may do it middling often. May God bless and keep you all!

"Your Affectionate Husband and Father,

"JOHN BROWN."

This letter shows that none of the Brown family (who had numbered fourteen in the early summer of 1856, all living within a few miles of Osawatomie) remained in that Territory in October, except Frederick, who had been buried near where he was murdered, August 30. His funeral was held at the house of his aunt, Mrs. S. L. Adair, the half-sister of John Brown. Mr. Adair was a missionary preacher, at whose log-cabin the Browns often lodged, in that and later years. Their own cabins had been burned and their growing crops destroyed by invaders from Missouri. Mr. Day was a relative of Mrs. John Brown, and had a cabin near the Browns. I visited the spot in after years, and found a few of the fruit trees planted by Jason Brown still standing and bearing fruit.

Those members of the family not named in the letter were Ruth Thompson, the eldest daughter, whose husband, Henry Thompson, badly wounded in June, was going back to the Adirondac woods, and Salmon and Oliver, eldest and youngest sons of the second marriage, who were on their way thither. Watson, their brother, met his father in Iowa, on his way to join the fighters in Kansas, and turned back with his brothers. I saw all these men except Oliver, who was then with his father in Iowa, at the North Elba farmhouse, in August, 1857, when I went there on an errand soon to be related. Thompson recovered from his wound, and is yet living, though a great invalid, in Pasadena, California. Jason is living with his son in Akron, Ohio, at the age of 86, and "Wealthy," Mrs. John Brown, Jr., is living with her children at Put-in-

Bay, an island in Lake Erie, where her home has been for forty-six years.

The head of this great family, almost a clan by itself, reached Chicago about October 24, and was there met and cared for by the National Kansas Committee, whom I had met in August. He was still wearing the summer garments in which he had fought his Kansas battles; but was taken in charge by Horace White, and fitted out, at the cost of the committee, with a full winter suit of brown, giving him the look of a New England deacon. But he wore a military stock and gray overcoat, which sustained his common title of "Captain Brown," by which we all knew him for the rest of his days. It was due to his air and habit of command; but it was also a title regularly conferred in December, 1855, by Major-General Charles Robinson and Brigadier-General Jim Lane, as the following certificate in my possession, with its autograph signatures, may show:

"HEADQUARTERS, KANSAS VOLUNTEERS,
"LAWRENCE CITY, December 11, 1855.

"This is to certify that John Brown Jr. faithfully and gallantly served as private in the Liberty Guards, Kansas Volunteers, from the 27th day of November, 1855, to the 13th day of December, 1855, in defending the city of Lawrence in Kansas Territory, from demolition by foreign invaders; when he was honorably discharged from said service.   "JOHN BROWN, Captain.

"[Countersigned]

"GEORGE W. SMITH, Col. Com'g 5th Regt. Kansas Vols.

"J. H. LANE, Gen, 1st Brig. Kansas Vols.

"C. ROBINSON, Maj. Gen."

As Captain Brown and his sons all became "Liberty Guards" at the same time, they had been in the service fourteen days. In Lawrence, however, they had arrived in the forenoon of December 7— Brown and four of his sons only. Jason and Oliver, with Henry Thompson, his son-in-law, had been ill at Jason's camp, eight miles northwest of Osawatomie, and were unable to march. George W. Brown, who has written copiously on all sides of the Kansas questions and drawn much on his imagination, says he saw Brown and his party arrive a little before sunset, seven in number—there were actually five—and about December 3, three days before they appeared. He then adds, in substance:

"As the party dismounted [from a lumber wagon] I grasped the hands of John and Frederick Brown, who introduced me to their father and brothers. [These were Owen and Salmon Brown.] I took the whole family to the rooms of the Committee of Safety and introduced them. Here, at my suggestion, John Brown was first clothed with the title of Captain, conferred on him by Governor Robinson, and approved by the Committee of Public Safety."

Brown was introduced to his Massachusetts friends by this title, and to the Massachusetts Legislature by me in the February following his introduction to me. Soon after this legislative hearing, at which Brown spoke, he visited me in Concord (March, 1856), where I was then living at the house of my poet-friend, Ellery Channing, on the Main Street, opposite the home of the Thoreau family. Mr. Channing himself was living in New Bedford, engaged in editing the *Mercury* newspaper, and the whole house was at my disposal, except the rooms occupied by his faithful housekeeper, Ann Carney, who also acted in that capacity for my sister Sarah. I therefore gave Brown the spare chamber which Mr. Channing, when at home, reserved for his own visitors, and took him with me at noon, across the street, to dine at Mrs. Thoreau's table, where I was then dining daily, and where some of my pupils were boarding. All Concord had heard the year before of Brown's fights and escapes in Kansas; and Thoreau, who had his own bone to pick with the civil government, which he had resisted while at Walden, and had gone to prison rather than pay a tax to uphold slavery, was desirous of meeting Brown. My school at this time claimed part of my attention, for young Abbot, though a fine scholar, had not the gift of authority; and at two o'clock I left Brown and Thoreau discussing Kansas affairs in Mrs. Thoreau's dining-room, or in the parlor, in which, five years after, Thoreau died. Brown narrated in detail to Thoreau his most noted battle in Kansas—that of Black Jack, the June before, where, with nine men, he captured twenty-odd men under the command of Henry Clay Pate, of Virginia. In this surrender he took charge of Captain Pate's " side-arms," and among others, a magnificently mounted Bowie-knife, presented to Pate by his friends in Virginia, when he started out to

subjugate the wicked abolitionists who had pre-
sumed to migrate to Kansas, and there oppose
negro slavery. To me also, in the evening after,
as we sat by my fire in the Channing house, Brown
related the story of this capture, and when he mentioned the knife, I said, "What became of that?"
Brown gravely pulled up the right leg of his ker-
seymere trousers, above the top of his high boot,
and drew from that crypt the sheathed knife which
Pate had worn in another part of his outfit. It was
the blade of this formidable knife which, the following spring, served as pattern for the thousand
pike-heads made for Brown at Collinsville in Connecticut.

While Thoreau and Brown sat thus conversing
in the early afternoon of a short winter day, Emerson, who had returned from his Western lecture-
tour, came up, as he often did, to call on Thoreau,
and was introduced by him to John Brown. He
invited Brown to his own house, where Brown
spent the second night of this two-days' visit at
Concord. Or rather, the Emerson house being full,
he took Brown to lodge at the ancient farmhouse
of the late Deacon Brown, now the Antiquarian
Museum, where Emerson hired a large room for
his own use when he sought retirement, and for his
visitors of the night, if the beds were occupied
at home. From the conversation at Thoreau's
(now the home of Mr. Alcott's grandson, Frederick Pratt), and from the longer intercourse of
Saturday night, when Brown was Emerson's guest,
came to Emerson and Thoreau that intimate knowl-

edge of Brown's character and general purpose
which qualified them, in October, 1859, to make
those addresses in his behalf which were the first
response among American scholars to the heroism
of the man who, in Emerson's striking phrase,
"made the gallows glorious like the Cross." But
Emerson had long been attentive to what was going wrong in Kansas and in the nation at large.
He had given $50 to aid the Free State men in
May, '56, and he had consented to speak to his
Harvard College friends in September, at the invitation of our Middlesex County Committee, of
which one of the college faculty, James Jennison,
had become a member. The call for this meeting,
which was not very largely attended, as I cut it
from the Cambridge *Chronicle* at the time, is this:

" AID FOR KANSAS.

" The Inhabitants of Cambridge, of all sects and
parties, who desire that peace, with free institutions, may
be established in Kansas, are invited to meet at Lyceum
Hall on Wednesday evening, Sept. 10, at 7 1-2 o'clock,
to consider the present condition of the inhabitants of
that Territory, and what aid we can properly afford them
in this time of their trial and suffering.

" RALPH WALDO EMERSON will address the meet-
ig. E. B. Whitman, Esq., our fellow citizen, is expected
from Lawrence, [K. T.] with late and reliable news, but
should he not arrive, other gentlemen recently from
Kansas, will be present and give information concerning
the management of the funds already collected, the present necessities of the people and their prospects for the

future, with other matters relating to the Territory, of interest to every humane and patriotic citizen.

" Several gentlemen of Cambridge, who never speak but to delighted ears, are engaged to give their voices to the cause of Free Kansas, on this occasion.

" Let us ' strengthen the things which remain and are ready to die.' By request of the Middlesex County
                                    Kansas Fund Committee."

In course of his short address, Emerson had this pungent criticism on the courts of Kansas under the appointment of President Pierce of New Hampshire:

" The President told a Kansas committee that the whole difficulty there grew ' from the factious spirit of the Kansas people respecting institutions which they need not have concerned themselves about.' A very remarkable speech from a Democratic President to his fellow citizens— that they are not to concern themselves with institutions which they alone are to create and determine. If that be Government, extirpation is the only cure. . . . In the free States we give a sniveling support to Slavery. The judges give cowardly interpretations to the law, in direct opposition to the known foundation of all law—that *every immoral statute is void.* And here of Kansas the President says, ' Let the complainants go to the courts "; though he knows that when the poor plundered farmer comes to the court, he finds the ringleader who has robbed him dismounting from his own horse, *and unbuckling his knife to sit as his judge.*"

I was present at this Cambridge meeting in my capacity as secretary of the Middlesex Committee,

and I preserved a saying of Emerson's that did not
get into his manuscript. It illustrates how he could
be more concise than that marvel of compression
in his rhetoric, Tacitus, the Roman historian.
Speaking of the absence, from the champions of
slavery and the defenders of legalized anarchy in
Kansas, of the great authorities in law and morals,
he said it was like the omission from the funeral of
Junia of the images of Brutus and Cassius, of
which Tacitus had said:

" *Eo ipso praefulgebant quod non visebantur* ";

adding in a swift version of the pregnant Latin,
" They glared out of their absences."

CHAPTER IV

Concord and North Elba

THE speech made by Brown in Concord, Saturday evening, in March, 1857, has been confounded, in Dr. Edward Emerson's notes to his father's Boston speech on Brown, with Brown's later one, made Saturday or Sunday evening in May, 1859, in which he told the story of his invasion of Missouri in the Christmas holidays of 1858, bringing away a dozen slaves, emancipated by force, a little more than two years before the Union army began to follow Brown's example in this respect. It was for his speech of 1857 that Brown brought with him the trace-chain with which his son John had been bound in Kansas, and made to keep up with the mounted men who were carrying him to his imprisonment at Lecompton, from which he had only been released a few weeks when he accompanied his father to Tabor, as mentioned in the letter just quoted. Both the chain and the Bowie-knife were shown by him in 1857, but only the knife in 1859. But Dr. Emerson, then a schoolboy under my instruction, has preserved one recollection of the evening at his father's house, when, as he says:

" Brown told of his experiences as a sheep-farmer, and his eye for animals and power over them. He said he knew at once a strange sheep in his flock of many hundred, and that he could make a dog or cat so uncomfortable as to wish to leave the room—simply by fixing his eyes on it."

Several persons have heard from Brown his dealings with his flocks near Akron, Ohio, where he herded the sheep of Colonel Simon Perkins, but no one else, I think, has mentioned this hypnotic power over animals. In 1878 I visited Colonel Perkins, and questioned him about his relations with Brown, of which he was rather unwilling to talk. He was eight years younger than Brown, and like him, born of Connecticut parentage, but in northern Ohio; a man of wealth, who had lost money by his partnership with John Brown and misconceived his character in some points. I saw his great sheep-farm a mile west of Akron Station, and the plain farmhouse where Brown lived, across the road from the great stone mansion of Colonel Perkins. There, in 1844, Perkins kept 1500 sheep, of which for some years Brown and his sons had the care. The gruff old man told me, in May, 1878, that Brown "was a rough herdsman, but a nice judge of wool; the shepherd dogs which he used did more harm than good, but they were in fashion then." He added that Brown had not much experience in sheep-raising when he took charge of the Perkins flock, and did not at first take the best care of them. "He did not fellowship with any church very much, and always acted upon his own impulses—he would not listen to anybody." Such was the old capitalist's view. Emerson had quite another conception of Brown. He said at Salem (January 6, 1860):

" A shepherd and herdsman, he learned the manners of animals, and knew the secret signals by which animals communicate. He made his hard bed on the mountains with them; he learned to drive his flock through thickets all but impassable; he had all the skill of a shepherd, by choice of breed and by wise husbandry to obtain the best wool, and that for a course of years. If he kept sheep, it was with a royal mind; and if he traded in wool he was a merchant-prince—not in the amount of wealth, but in his protection of the interests confided to him."

No report was made of Brown's Concord speech in 1857, but Emerson in his journal preserved this passage: "One of his good points was the folly of the peace party in Kansas—who believed that their strength lay in the greatness of their wrongs, and so discountenanced resistance. Well, was their wrong greater than the negro slave's? and what kind of strength has that given to the negro?"

Thoreau's journal of Brown's first visit to Concord, and his conversation by the fireside, has disappeared, being included in his " Plea for Captain John Brown," the most of which he took from his journal pages, as his manner was, in writing speeches or essays. But he records several sayings of Brown's, which I heard at the table as we dined together. Others of the same tenor I had from Brown as we were driving or traveling together in Massachusetts or Pennsylvania. Thoreau says:

" I heard Brown say that his father was a contractor who furnished beef to the army in the War with England in 1812; that he accompanied his father to the camp, seeing a good deal of military life; more, perhaps, than if he had been a soldier, for he was often present at the councils of officers. Especially he learned by experience how armies are supplied and maintained in the field—a work which, he observed, required at least as much experience and skill as to lead them in battle. Few persons, he said, had any conception of the cost, even the pecuniary cost, of firing a single bullet in war. He saw enough in that war to disgust him with a military life—indeed, to excite in him a great abhorrence of it. So much so that though he was tempted by the offer of some petty office in the army, when he was about 18, he not only declined that, but also refused to ' train ' when ' warned ' and was fined for it. He resolved then not to have anything to do with any war, unless it were a war for liberty.

" When he went to Europe in the wool-business, there, as everywhere, he had his eyes about him, and made many original observations. He saw, for instance, why the soil of England was so rich, and that of Germany so poor; it was because the peasantry in England live on the soil which they cultivate, while in Germany they are gathered into villages at night.*

" As for his tact and prudence—at a time when scarcely a man from the Free States was able to reach Kansas, by any direct route, at least, without having his arms taken from him, Brown, carrying what imperfect guns and other weapons he could collect, openly and slowly

---

* What Brown said to me on this topic was, that this retiring from the fields to sleep in the villages, with their cattle and horses, was " taking the natural manures away from the soil " in German and Belgian rural districts. He also commented unfavorably on the Austrian soldiers, as contrasted with the French.

drove a cart through Missouri, apparently in the character of a surveyor, with his surveying compass exposed in it; and so passed unsuspected, and had ample opportunity to learn the designs of the enemy. When I expressed surprise that he could live in Kansas, with so large a number exasperated against him (including the authorities), he accounted for it by saying, ' It is perfectly well understood that I will not be taken.' He could even come out into a town where there were more Border Ruffians than Free-State men, and transact some business (without delaying long) and yet not be molested. For, said he, ' No handful of men were willing to undertake it, and a large body could not be got together in season.' In his camp, as I myself heard him state, he permitted no profanity, and no man of loose morals was suffered to remain there, unless as a prisoner of war. ' I would rather,' said he, ' have the small-pox, yellow fever and cholera altogether in my camp, than men without principle. Give me men of good principles—God-fearing men—men who respect themselves; and with a dozen of them I will oppose any hundred such men as those Buford ruffians.' And I noticed that he did not overstate anything, but spoke within bounds. I remember particularly how, in his speech at the Town Hall, he referred to what his family had suffered in Kansas, without ever giving the least vent to his pent-up fire. It was a volcano with an ordinary chimney-flue. Referring to the deeds of certain Border Ruffians, he said, rapidly paring away his speech, like an experienced soldier, keeping a reserve of force and meaning—' They had a perfect right to be hung.' "

Brown had in his mind then, no doubt, the five victims of his Pottawatomie executions, although they were not specially mentioned; he was also thinking of such as gave illegal votes from Missouri in 1855-56. After this visit to Concord, about March 15, Brown went to Worcester, where he spoke at a public meeting, March 23, 1857, and visited Eli Thayer, in his " Oread Castle," where for some years Mr. Thayer had kept a school for girls, from which he withdrew in 1857, after his election to Congress in November, 1856.*

Of Brown's appearance and mode of public speech at Worcester, President Wayland's son, Rev. H. L. Wayland, then a Baptist pastor in Worcester, wrote as follows, several years after Brown's death:

" In the spring of 1857, just after the Dred Scott

* Eli Thayer was born in Mendon, Massachusetts, June 11, 1819, and died in Worcester, April 15, 1899. He was graduated at Brown University in 1845, and in the same year began teaching in the Worcester Academy. While thus occupied he began to build his " Oread Institute " on a hill not far from that Academy, in 1848; and in the first tower of that building he opened a private school for girls in May, 1849, of which he remained the Principal until he retired in 1857,—still continuing to own the " Oread Castle " and to reside there when living in Worcester. In 1854, while a member of the General Court of Massachusetts, he organized the New England Emigrant Aid Company, and was active in its promotion and administration until elected to Congress in November, 1856. He served two terms at Washington (1857-1861), but was defeated for a third term at the election of 1860. His school continued until 1881, but he did not direct it as Principal after leaving Congress; nor did his active interest in Kansas affairs continue beyond 1858. He then had a scheme for attacking slavery in Virginia by colonization, as in Kansas, and he made a beginning at a place in what is now West Virginia, which he called " Ceredo." But this did not long flourish, and was finally ended by the Civil War. He was for a short time a treasury agent under Secretary Chase in 1861 and 1862, and in the latter year proposed to Secretary Stanton an emigration scheme for Florida, and other abortive plans for coloniza-

decision of the Supreme Court, I, being then a resident of Worcester, was getting up a lecture for Frederick Douglass, at which the then mayor of the city, for the first time in an American city, presided at an address of Mr. Douglass. I called at the house of Eli Thayer, afterwards member of Congress from that District, to ask him to sit on the platform. Here I found a stranger, a man of tall, gaunt form, with a face smooth-shaven, destitute of the full beard that later became a part of history. The children were climbing over his knees; he said, ' The children always come to me.' I was then introduced to John Brown of Osawatomie. How little one imagined then that within less than three years the name of this plain home-spun man would fill America and Europe! Mr. Brown consented to occupy a place on the platform, and at the urgent request of the audience spoke briefly. It is one of the curious facts, that many men who *do* it are utterly unable to *tell* about it. John Brown, a flame of fire in action, was dull in speech."

The visit at Worcester, where Brown was the guest of Eli Thayer, followed his visit to me at Concord, and in consequence of these notes from Mr. Thayer, Congressman-elect from the Worcester district:

tion in Utah and South America. From 1864 to 1870 he was land agent for a railroad in Missouri, with an office in New York, but still had his family residence at "Oread" in Worcester. He left that home a short time before his death. During the eight years or more that he was Principal of his Institute, about two hundred girls were his pupils, by whom he is described as a good Latin scholar and a strict disciplinarian. A history (New Haven, 1905) of the school, under its successive Principals, has been published by Mrs. Martha Burt Wright of New Haven, giving sketches of Mr. Thayer, his pupils and their teachers. A manuscript biography of Mr. Thayer was prepared by Mr. Franklin P. Rice of Worcester some years since, which awaits publication.

" WORCESTER, March 18, 1857.

" *Friend Brown:*

" I have just returned from Albany, and find your favor of the 16th. I am glad you had a good meeting at Concord—as I knew you would have, for the blood of heroes is not extinct in that locality. I will see some of our friends here to-morrow, and we will decide at once about your speaking here. If you are to speak, you will do well to be here a day or two in advance, and converse with some of our citizens. I will write you again to-morrow.

" March 19.—I have seen some of our friends to-day, and they say you had better come here next Monday. There is to be an anti-slavery meeting in the evening, and I think it will be a very good time for you to present your cause—which is the Free-State cause of Kansas, which is the cause of mankind. I shall expect you to do me the favor of stopping at my house.

" Truly yours,

" ELI THAYER."

Upon both these letters is this indorsement in the handwriting of John Brown: " Eli Thayer. Answered March 23d in person." This means that he went to Worcester that day, and in the evening met Dr. Wayland. A week later I was with Brown at the house of A. H. Reeder, the first Governor of Kansas, where I met Brown and Martin Conway, and with our united arguments, we tried to persuade Mr. Reeder to return to Kansas as the agent of the Kansas committees, and take the head of the Free State party there, in place of Charles Robinson, who had lost the confidence of many men, there and in the East. How serious this affair was may be seen by the letter of Augustus Wattles to John Brown in the following summer. Writing from Lawrence, August 21, 1857, Wattles said:

" I think Dr. Robinson's failure to meet the legislature last winter disheartened the people so that they lost confidence in him and in the movement. Although in the Convention we invited him to withdraw his resignation (which he did), yet the masses could never be vitalized again into that enthusiasm and confidence which they had before. Another mistake which he made, equally fatal, was his attack upon George W. Brown and the " Herald of Freedom "; thus leading off his friends into a party by themselves, and leaving all who doubted and hated him in another party."

When thus meeting Brown and Conway at Easton, I was on my return from a first visit to Washington, in the early days of Buchanan's administration; but I had met there only a few personal friends, Congress not being in session.   At Philadelphia, either going or returning, I held a long interview with J. W. Geary, lately returned from his honorable but displaced post as Governor of Kansas, and full of wrath at the treatment he had received from President Pierce, who had appointed him, and from President Buchanan, in whose interest as candidate Geary had accepted the appointment, seven months before. He was at the Continental Hotel, with his secretary, Dr. Gihon, who soon after published a book about the Kansas troubles, and I called on them there. I found Geary a frank, vain person, whose self-complacency had suffered cruel mortification, and who had deserved a better treatment than he got, either from the pro-slavery administration or from our Free State friends, to whom, as I have mentioned, he had done good service, and, on the whole, given fair play. He afterward was a brave soldier on the Union side in the Civil War; but I never saw him again.

We spent the whole afternoon at Governor Reeder's comfortable village house in Easton, and put our case fairly before him. Judge Conway spoke in the name of the few Free State lawyers in Kansas; I spoke for the Massachusetts Kansas Committee, as I had authority to do; and John Brown offered his services as commander of men in partisan warfare, should that be needful. Reeder heard us courteously, gave us the facts concerning his troubled career in the Territory, and showed courage and good sense in his conversation, as he had in his conduct while Governor. But he said that his personal interests had suffered by his absence in Kansas; that he must reconstruct his practice as a lawyer, and that his first duty was to his family and neighbors in Pennsylvania. We could not deny this; he had been worse treated than Geary, and we ceased to urge him. Brown and I returned to New York, and Conway, I believe, went to visit his friends in Maryland. From Easton, March 29, Brown wrote to Thayer at Worcester, suggesting aid for his company of Kansas irregular cavalry, in raising which Thayer fully sympathized. He wrote to Brown in the most friendly tone, March 30, and told him that the Worcester County Committee would give him, through Colonel Higginson, $50 for his campaign. Again (April 17) Thayer wrote, partly in regard to his own rather futile scheme of colonizing West Virginia with anti-slavery men, and said:

" Will you allow me to suggest a name for your company? I should call them 'the Neighbors,' from Luke, tenth chapter: ' Which thinkest thou was *neighbor* to him who fell among thieves? '

" Our Virginia scheme is gaining strength wonderfully. Every mail brings me offers of land and men. The press universally favors it—that is, so far as we care for favor. It is bound to go ahead. You must have a home in Western Virginia."

In the meantime I had returned to Concord and Boston, and on the 15th of April, 1857, as a member of the Executive Committee, of which G. L. Stearns, Dr. S. G. Howe, Thomas Russell and one or two others were members with me, I moved and recorded these votes—a previous vote of the whole State Kansas Committee having given Brown the custody of our 200 Sharpe's rifles at Tabor and voted him $500 for the expense of taking and caring for them:

BOSTON, April 15, 1857.
" At a meeting of the executive committee of the State Kansas Aid Committee of Massachusetts, held in Boston, April 11, 1857, it was

" *Voted,* That Captain John Brown be authorized to dispose of one hundred rifles, belonging to this committee, to such Free-State inhabitants of Kansas as he thinks to be reliable, at a price not less than fifteen dollars; and that he account for the same agreeably to his instructions, for the relief of Kansas.

" At the same meeting it was

" *Voted,* That Captain John Brown be authorized to draw on P. T. Jackson, treasurer, for five hundred dollars, if on his arrival in Kansas he is satisfied that such sum is necessary for the relief of persons in Kansas."

Brown had already received from members of our committee, and from others, so much property, that, in view of his taking the rifles also, he sat down in Boston, April 13, with his good friends, the Russells and Rev. Daniel Foster, and made the following provisional will for the protection of the property, in case of accident to him:

" I, John Brown, of North Elba, N. Y., intending to visit Kansas, and knowing the uncertainty of life, make my last will as follows: I give and bequeath all trust funds and personal property for the aid of the Free-State cause in Kansas, now in my hands or in the hands of W. H. D. Callender, of Hartford, Conn., to George L. Stearns, of Medford, Mass., Samuel Cabot, Jr., of Boston, Mass., and William H. Russell, of New Haven, Conn., to them and the survivor or survivors and their assigns forever, in trust that they will administer said funds and other property, including all now collected or hereafter to be collected by me or in my behalf for the aid of the Free-State cause in Kansas, leaving the manner of so doing entirely at their discretion.

" Signed at Boston, Mass., this 13th day of April,
A. D., 1857, in presence of us, who, in presence of said
Brown and of each other, have at his request affixed our
names as witnesses of his will. The words ' and personal
property' and ' and other property' interlined before
signature by said Brown, and ' said Callender,' erased.

                                "(Signed)   JOHN BROWN.

" DANIEL FOSTER,
" MARY ELLEN RUSSELL,
" THOMAS RUSSELL,
                    " *Witnesses.*"

During this visit of Brown to various parts of
New England, New York and Pennsylvania, I saw
much of him and of those who aided him in his
general purpose of freeing Kansas, and ultimately
the whole country, from negro slavery. His visit
and his tours lasted for three or four months, and
I was with him not only in Concord and Boston,
but at New York, in a meeting of the National
Kansas Committee, and in other places. This gave
me opportunity to see him under many circumstances, and to form my opinion of his extraor-
dinary character—an opinion that I have had no
occasion to change. Among those who also saw
much of him at this time was Mr. Amos Lawrence,
father of the present Bishop Lawrence. He, like
Eli Thayer and Charles Robinson, seemed to have
the same friendship and admiration for Brown that
I had. The day after Brown's address to the
members of the Massachusetts Legislature in February, and again a month later, Mr. Lawrence, at

whose house he had been a guest, wrote to Brown in these terms:

" Boston, Feb. 19, 1857.

" *My Dear Sir:*

" Enclosed you will find seventy dollars. Please write to John Conant, of East Jaffrey, N. H., and acknowledge receipt; or write to me saying you have received the Jaffrey money, and I will send your letter to them. It is for your own personal use, and not for the cause in any other way than that. I am sorry not to have seen you before you left. It may not be amiss to say that you may find yourself disappointed if you rely on the National Kansas Committee for any considerable amount of money. Please to consider this as confidential; and it is only my own opinion, without *definite* knowledge of their operations.

(*Private.*)

" Boston, March 20, 1857.

" *My Dear Sir:*

" Your letter from New Haven is received. I have just sent to Kansas near fourteen thousand dollars to establish a fund to be used, first, to secure the best system of common schools for Kansas that exists in this country; second, to establish Sunday schools. The property is held by two trustees in Kansas, and cannot return to me. On this account, and because I am always short of money, I have not the cash to use for the purpose you name. But in case anything should occur, while you are engaged in a great and good cause, to shorten your life, you may be assured that your wife and children shall be cared for more liberally than you now propose. The family of ' Captain John Brown of Osawatomie ' will not be turned out to starve in this country, until Liberty herself is driven out.

" I hope you will not run the risk of arrest. Come and see me when you have time."

Mr. Lawrence also undertook, with the aid of others, to raise $1,000 for the purchase of land at North Elba, to increase the home comfort of the wife and daughter of Brown, then living in the Adirondac forest with great simplicity and home. liness in their surroundings. Upon this matter, the following facts are interesting:

At this time, of course, neither Mr. Lawrence, Mr. Stearns, Gerrit Smith, nor myself had any knowledge of the plan of Brown for a campaign in Virginia, but we were all willing that he should, under sufficient provocation, and for the better pro-tection of our friends in Kansas, make incursions into Missouri. The subscription paper, drawn up by Mr. Lawrence, with its signatures, was as follows:

" The family of Captain John Brown of Osawatomie have no means of support, owing to the oppression to which he has been been subjected in Kansas Territory. It is proposed to put them (his wife and five children) in possession of the means of supporting themselves, so far as is possible for persons in their situation. The under-signed, therefore, will pay the following sums, provided one thousand dollars should be raised. With this sum a small farm can now be purchased in the neighborhood of their late residence in Essex County, New York."

May, '57. Paid. William R. Lawrence, Fifty dollars.

Paid. Amos A. Lawrence, $\left.\begin{array}{l}\text{one hundred dollars.}\\ \$235 \text{ more.}\\ \overline{}\\ \$335\end{array}\right\}$

Paid. George L. Stearns, $\left.\begin{array}{l}\text{Fifty dollars.}\\ \$235 \text{ more.}\\ \overline{}\\ \$285\end{array}\right\}$

Paid. John E. Lodge, twenty-five dollars.
Paid. J. Carter Brown [by A. A. L.], one hundred dollars.
Paid. J. M. S. Williams, fifty dollars.
Paid. John Bertram [by M. S. W.], seventy-five dollars.
Paid. W. D. Pickman, fifty dollars.
Paid. R. P. Waters [by W. D. P.], ten dollars.
Paid. S. E. Peabody, ten dollars.
Paid. John H. Silsbee, ten dollars.
Paid. B. Silsbee, five dollars.
Paid. Cash, ten dollars.
Paid. Wendell Phillips, twenty-five dollars.
Paid. W. J. Rotch, ten dollars.
Paid. George L. Stearns, two hundred and thirty-five dollars.
Paid. A. A. Lawrence, two hundred and thirty-five dollars.
One thousand dollars in all. July 27, 1857.

Boston, Nov. 5. 1857. John Bertram's subscription being $75, instead of $25, as I supposed, I have returned to Amos A. Lawrence twenty-five dollars, making his whole subscription $310; my subscription $260; all others $430; total $1000.

(Signed)   George L. Stearns.

The subscription thus raised was expended in completing the purchase of a tract, originally sold by Gerrit Smith to the brothers of Henry Thompson (Brown's son-in-law), but which had not been wholly paid for. In August, 1857, as the agent of

Messrs. Stearns and Lawrence, I visited North
Elba, examined the land, paid the Thompsons their
stipulated price for improvements, and to Mr.
Smith the remainder of the purchase money, took
the necessary deeds, and transferred the property
to Mrs. Brown and Mrs. Thompson, according to
the terms arranged by Captain Brown in the preceding spring. I preserved this pencil memoran-
dum, in Gerrit Smith's familiar handwriting, showing this transaction:

Draft of F. B. S.		$1000
Due Thompsons	$574	
Due me on note	111.66	
" " on land	288.89	974.55
		$25.45

This sum ($25.45) I handed to Mrs. Brown at
North Elba, August 13, 1857. A few days later
I reported to Mr. Stearns as follows:

" I wrote you from Buffalo, I think, telling you of the
settling of the business of Captain Brown with Mr.
Smith; since when I have been in North Elba, and passed
a night under his roof. There I found Mrs. Brown, a
tall, large woman, fit to be the mother of heroes, as she
is. Her family are her two sons and three daughters, one
of them a child of three years. One of the sons has been
in Kansas; the other was to go with his father this summer, but I think his marriage, which took place in April,
may have prevented it. Owen is now with his father,
and both, I suppose, are in Kansas, for on the 17th of
July they were beyond Iowa City with their teams. I
shall have much to tell you about this visit. The subscription could not have been better bestowed, and the
small balance, which I paid Mrs. Brown, came very op-
portunely."

The final subscription of Mr. Lawrence to this fund was $310, that of Mr. Stearns, $260. My subscription was my traveling expenses—about $50, I think, for I kept no close account. I first went to Peterboro, in Madison County, N. Y., the birthplace and baronial home of Mr. Smith; then, after cashing the draft for $1,000 and paying him, I took the balance for the Thompson brothers, and renewed a visit to Niagara, which I first made the summer before; then went down the Niagara and the St. Lawrence to Montreal, passing through the Lachine Rapids under the pilotage of the famous boatman, Baptiste—and from Montreal went by rail to Burlington, as my neighbor Thoreau had done seven years before. From Burlington, Vt., I steamed up the lake (Champlain) and across it to Keeseville, where I landed and went inland to Au Sable Forks, to spend the night, and the next morning early, hired a "buckboard" (primitive one-seated wagon) and drove myself through the towns of Wilmington and Jay, and through the romantic Wilmington Pass, to the frame house of John Brown in North Elba, a few miles east of Lake Placid. It was then not much more than a frame, boarded and clapboarded, and much of it lathed, but with only two or three plastered rooms. It was on the very edge of the forest, and Watson and Salmon Brown, when I arrived, were getting the logs together and burning them to extend the "clearing" which they had "cut off," a little farther from the house, along the rude highway. The house then sheltered Mrs. Brown and five of her children, for Oliver was absent, but not in Connecti-

cut, where his father had placed him in April.
Ruth, the only surviving daughter of the first marriage, was living with her husband, Henry Thompson, in a smaller house, across the pasture, for which
I had come to pay his brothers. The women of
both families were gathering and drying the wild
red raspberry, then ripening abundantly, so that
they might make sauce and pies with them in the
long, cold winter.

I was the guest of these worthy people for two
nights and a day, during which I transacted the
needful business, heard from Henry Thompson the
story of his adventures in Kansas, and on the way
there; and of the fight at Black Jack, where he
was wounded, and still carried the rifle ball in his
muscular frame—for it was not extracted till years
afterward. Ruth Thompson entertained me with
anecdotes of her father, and with her own cheerful
and friendly nature. Indeed, the whole family
seemed to be cheerful in the midst of poverty and
anxieties, such as few households then felt; a manly
and womanly resolution and generosity prevailed,
characteristic of these remarkable households.
Henry Thompson wrote out for me, years after,
the story that he told me in his homestead then,
and I will insert it here, for I think it has never
been printed. He was afterward a pioneer in Wisconsin, and a citizen of Pasadena in California. He
was born in New Hampshire, and had the traits of
that hardy State. The town of Keene, below North
Elba, on the way to Westport and civilization, was
named for the New Hampshire Keene, from which
some of its pioneers had come.

STATEMENT OF HENRY THOMPSON

(Formerly of N. Elba, N. Y.)

CONCERNING HIS KANSAS EXPERIENCES, 1855-56.

(Dictated to His Daughter, December, 1900.)

About August 15, 1855, I left North Elba, where I had married Ruth Brown, and joined John Brown at Hudson, O., where his father was then living. We went on a Saturday by boat from Cleveland to Detroit, where we stayed over Sunday, and heard Alexander Campbell, founder of the Campbellite Christians, preach; then went to Chicago, whither we had sent our freight. There we bought a young horse, and packed our freight into a "democrat" wagon; it consisted of firearms, a tent, blankets, provisions, surveying tools, etc. My brother-in-law, Oliver Brown, joined us at Chicago. Thence we started across Illinois in a southwesterly direction, as nearly in a straight line as we could, for Rock Island on the Mississippi. We crossed the river there, kept our course across the southeast corner of Iowa, and struck the Missouri River at a little place called Brunswick, in Chariton County, Missouri, about midway of the State from east to west—now a town of 2,000 people. The most conspicuous building there in 1855 was a slave-pen. While we waited for a ferry-boat to take us across, an old man came out to us, looked us over and asked, "Where are you going" Capt. Brown said, "To Kansas." "Where from?" "New York." The old man said, "You will not live to get there." Brown's reply was, "We are prepared not to die alone." The Missourian seemed to lose interest, and said no more.

We traveled some days without incident, moving westward. When we got to Lexington, also on the Missouri, we stopped at a hotel to feed our horse and look around a little. About a dozen men were in the barroom; one of whom, telling about his going to Kansas that year with Gov. Reeder, said that whenever they came to a little hamlet the Governor would stop and make a speech; but when they came to Lawrence, he never gave it a passing nod; and they rode away so hard that " they killed a me-are and a me-ule." Going out to look the town over, we went towards the river, and overtook a gang of slaves who were being taken to the river to be sent South. We saw them put aboard the steamer for St. Louis. Poor fellows, they looked as though " Forced from home and all its pleasures." We kept on westward, up the river, to a little town called Waverley, in Lafayette County, where Jason had buried his little son Austin, who died with cholera as he and John Brown, Jr., were going to Kansas the year before. We took up the coffin and carried it to where Jason was living, nine miles from Osawatomie.

As we neared the west border of Missouri, I noticed lots of men going westward; and one day a big crowd came along on horses and mules—each man carrying a double-barreled shotgun. I said to them, " Boys, where are you going? " " To Kansas; there is to be an election there next week, and we are going over to vote." " Why do you carry your shotguns? " " Oh, we might see some rattlesnakes, or some abolitionists."

We kept on about the same west course until we crossed the border into Kansas, at a little place, then called (I think) Santa Fé, a few miles south of Kansas City. Then we changed our course a little to the northwest, crossed the Osage River at Stanton, below Osawatomie, and found John and Jason with their families, out on the bald prairie at " Brown's Station," as John had christened it. We soon helped them build winter quarters in the timber. We arrived October 6, 1855, and had the families sheltered before December. Then came on the Wakarusa war. We heard the Missourians were coming over to burn Lawrence, and the leading men there sent for help. I could not go, as I was sick with ague. The rest of our company went—John, Owen, Frederick, Salmon, and Oliver, with Capt. Brown.

The Missourians came in sight of Lawrence and halted. Capt. Brown wanted to go out and give them battle; he said it would have a good effect to let a little blood. But the leading men would not hear of it; they said it would not take well in the East. Thus ended the war in 1855.

Our company all went to the election at Pottawatomie precinct in the fall of 1855; all went off quietly. As we started back for home, I happened to be in company with old man Doyle (afterwards killed near Dutch Henry's) and with others. Doyle was talking about the Southern slaves; said they were nothing but brutes; they did not know anything. "Sell husband, wife or children," he said; "they did not care anything about it." I said, "Look here, old man! I've seen colored men as much smarter than you are as you are smarter than that little dog running along yonder." Doyle replied, "That is incendiary language, and you will have to pay for it yet." So when Judge Cato came along from Lecompton, and opened court at Dutch Henry's Crossing, Doyle swore out a warrant for my arrest. We heard of it, and concluded it would be a good thing for me to go over and give myself up—Salmon Brown going with me to carry the news back. In case they arrested me, the whole company was to come over in the morning, march into the court, and hand me a couple of revolvers; we would then adjourn the court summarily. But the court had weakened, Judge Cato had gone—and I heard no more about the warrant.

In the spring of 1856, as soon as the grass got high

enough for mules to live on, the Missourians started and got to Lawrence before we could, and destroyed the Free State Hotel. Hearing of this, we turned back and camped that night at Ottawa Jones's (the friendly Indian). Captain Brown saw that something decisive must be done, and called for volunteers. " Further this deponent saith not;" Shore and Townsley have told their stories, not agreeing in all points.

The last Sunday in May, 1856, we were at Prairie City with Captain Shore and some of his men, when a company of Missourians came out to sack the place. As they approached, Capt. Shore jumped up and halloed, " Sharpe's Rifles! " The two Missouri leaders were then so near they did not dare to turn back, and we captured them. The others turned and fled as fast as their beasts could carry them. We kept the leaders for a few hours; they said they were good Missourians, and we let them go. Soon after, on the 1st of June, word came to us that a company of 75 men were out looking for Old Brown. We at once started to look for them. But night came on, and we had to camp on the prairie. But we started as soon as we could see in the morning; found the Missourians before they had eaten breakfast, and when their supply of whiskey had given out (the night before). Consequently their courage was very low at the time. Their camp was in a ravine by a spring called " Black Jack," at the edge of an oak timber. When we got within 200 yards of them we commenced firing. When one of them got hit, he would go down the ravine, mount his horse, which was fastened there, and ride away. After we had been fighting about three hours, Capt. H. C. Pate, who commanded them, sent out a couple of men, before he came himself, with a flag of truce. Capt. Brown went out to meet them, and asked if either of them was their captain. Being answered " No," he said, " I will go down with you and see your Captain," who, by that time, was coming out to meet Brown. Before going forth, Brown ordered his men to follow the ravine down to the enemy's camp. The two captains meeting, Brown asked Pate if he had any propo- sition to make; who replied, " No, but I wanted to tell you I am working under orders of the Government." Cap- tain Brown said, " I know exactly what you are. I have a proposition to make—and that is, your immediate and unconditional surrender." Approaching Pate's men, then under a lieutenant, Brockett, the latter said, " I won't sur- render till my captain gives the order." Turning to Pate, Captain Brown said, " You give the order!" which he made haste to do, as Brown raised his revolver. Thus 26 pro-slavery men surrendered to nine abolitionists, and gave up their weapons. I still have Lieutenant Brockett's Sharpe's rifle, and a cartridge box marked " A. A. Coffee."

But at the surrender I was not present, for I had been severely wounded about the middle of the fight. As my arm was raised to load my gun, the ball struck my side, glanced on a rib, ran under the shoulder-blade, and followed down the thick muscle beside the backbone. When taken out, long afterward, it was nine inches from where it went in. Loss of blood and thirst for water compelled me to leave the ground. It was about a mile to the place where we had left our horses, and there was water. Going that way, I met Frederick Brown on horseback, told him I was wounded, and would like to take his horse and ride to where there was water. He got off, I got on—and then the light went out. I supposed I was about to faint, got off, and lay down, and my sight came back. Again I got on the horse, with the same result; whereupon I told Fred to take the horse—I would go on foot. Thus I got to the water, and took a drink, which revived me very much.

I filled a bottle with the water, took another horse, and rode to Howard Carpenter's, where I stayed two nights; and then went to Capt. Brown's camp, on Ottawa Creek, where we had been encamped before the fight. Carpenter lived near Prairie City, which has now disappeared as a town, being included in the present town of Palmyra. O. A. Carpenter was wounded in the fight. My own wound is still felt. I am a carpenter, but never after that wound could I turn a hand-augur without great pain; and at one time I was laid up for five months, unable to do a day's work. My last attack was September, 1900. The only relief I get at such times is by blistering.

Much has been said at times about Governor Robinson, now dead. I remember reading a newspaper report of his inaugural address as Governor of Kansas, in which he said, "If the blood of Dow, of Barber and of Brown is not enough to satisfy, more victims must be furnished." I also remember a report of the distribution of some money sent from Boston to help the Free State cause. Of this Captain Brown got $11, and I got $7; but in laying claim to damages for property lost in the sack of Lawrence, May, 1856, Gov. Robinson put in a bill for $13,000, for furniture said to be loaned by him to the Free State Hotel, which was destroyed, and for losses at his own house.*

* In copying the MS. of Henry Thompson, I have added a few details to make the statements clearer, and would call attention to one or two variations from the historical account. Mr. Thompson speaks of the firing at Black Jack as "about an hour." But Owen Brown and other eye-witnesses have told me what is stated in my book,—that the firing was kept up at intervals from early morning till early afternoon. I therefore think Mr. T. meant to say three hours, or something of that sort. If only an hour, then he was wounded only half an hour after the firing began,—which is improbable. The Mr. Carpenter engaged in the fight is registered by John Brown, in a manuscript book which he gave me as "O. A. Carpenter." Who was Howard Carpenter?—probably his brother. —F. B. S.

I afterward met Henry Thompson at Put-in-Bay, where he lived for a time, near John Brown, Jr. His daughter, Mary Thompson, to whom he dictated the above account, is a teacher in Pasadena. I remember her, a blue-eyed child, at Put-in-Bay Island, and have much corresponded with her and her mother since. Ruth Thompson died at Pasedena in 1906.

Returning to Lake Champlain and Keeseville, I stopped at Au Sable Forks the night of August 14, 1857, and wrote to Captain Brown of my visit to his family. He replied, from Tabor, Iowa (August 27), thus:

"MY DEAR FRIEND,—Your most welcome letter, from Au Sable Forks, is received. I cannot express the gratitude I feel to all the kind friends who contributed towards paying for the place at North Elba, after I had bought it, as I am thereby relieved from a very great embarrassment both with Mr. Smith and the young Thompsons; and also comforted with the feeling that my noble-hearted wife and daughters will not be driven either to beg or become a burden to my poor boys, who have nothing but their hands to begin with. I am under special obligation to you for going to look after them and cheer them in their homely condition. May God reward you all a thousand-fold! No language I have can express the satisfaction it affords me to feel that I have friends who will take the trouble to look after them and know the real condition of my family, while I am far away, perhaps never to return."

CHAPTER V

Virginia and Kansas

IN western Iowa, Brown, in the autumn and winter of 1857-58, began to drill his small company of men for service either in Kansas, Missouri, or Virginia, as Providence might direct. He had chosen for his drill-master an Englishman, Hugh Forbes, who had been a silk merchant in Siena before the Garibaldian campaigns of 1848-9; had taken part with Garibaldi and commanded Italian volunteers under that brilliant general. Upon his failure and escape from Italy, or soon after, Forbes seems to have left Italy, too, and for a time resided in Paris, but afterward came over to New York, where he led a shifty life, apart from his family, who remained in Paris, while he supported himself by giving fencing lessons. There Brown found him in the early part of 1857, and engaged him, with payment in advance, to go to the West and drill his men. Forbes was also to publish a manual for irregular soldiers, such as he had commanded in Italy, and to write appeals to the soldiers of the United States army, inviting them to join in an attempt to abolish slavery by force, as Stevens had done, in Kansas, after leaving the army. This part of Brown's plan was not communicated to his Boston friends, but was known to Gerrit Smith, at whose house Forbes had

JASON BROWN, 1875

MRS. RUTH BROWN THOMPSON
(*Eldest daughter of John Brown*)

F. B. SANBORN, ÆT 25

D. W. WILDER, ÆT 60

visited on his way to join Brown in 1857. Though
I afterward had reason to correspond with Forbes,
I never saw him, nor do I regret the fact. With
plenty of courage, and some other good qualities,
he was vainglorious, headstrong, and, in brief, what
the French term "impossible." When he rejoined
Garibaldi, in 1860, in the Sicilian and Neapolitan
campaign, his general was obliged to deprive him
of all command, so quarrelsome and impracticable
had he become. Brown had the same experience
with him two or three years earlier. From the slender resources of Brown in the spring of 1857 (before May 1), Forbes drew $600, a good part of
which he used for the support of his family in
Paris, and the passage back to France of the
daughter who had come to New York with him;
and he delayed setting out for Iowa until July. He
then went leisurely westward, and was at Peterboro, N. Y., a few weeks before I got there in
early August, 1857. Meantime, Brown was impa-
tiently expecting him at Tabor. Forbes joined him
there August 9, while I was arranging the North
Elba business; and he had quarreled and left him
early in November, alleging that he, Forbes, and
not Brown, ought to lead the forces against
slavery. He began to write abusive letters to
Charles Sumner, Dr. Howe and to me in December, to several of which I made answer January 15,
1858, saying, among other things:

" I became acquainted with Captain Brown a little more
than a year ago, and have since been his warm friend and

admirer. Being a member of the Massachusetts Kansas Committee, I interested myself with my colleagues in his behalf, and we furnished him with some five thousand dollars in arms and money. As a temporary member of the National Committee (Jan. 24, '57), I procured the passage of a resolution appropriating five thousand dollars from that committee also, of which, however, only five hundred dollars has been paid. I also introduced him to a public meeting of my townsmen, who raised something for him. In the summer I visited Mr. Gerrit Smith, and made arrangements with him for the settlement of property worth a thousand dollars on the wife and daughter of Captain Brown. The money was raised in Boston by the men whom you calumniate. I visited the families in the wilderness where they live, and arranged the transfer of property. Mr. Smith first mentioned your name to me— unless it were a member of his family, Mr. Morton. Captain Brown had never done so, nor did any one hint to me that there was any agreement between you and him of the kind you mention. I think I wrote to Brown from Peterboro', informing him that you were at Davenport, having seen your letter to Mr. Smith announcing that fact. On September 14 I received Mr. Smith's letter, asking that some money be raised for your family, but merely on general grounds. I was pledged to aid and support Brown, and could not give money to persons of whom I knew little or nothing. Had Brown or yourself informed me of your agreement, the case would have been different. I kept Mr. Smith's draft just a week, returning it to him September 21; it was out of his hands just eleven days. Since then, I have had a few letters from Brown, and have seen some from you, but have heard nothing of any compact. To answer Brown's call for 'secret service' money, I procured about six hundred dollars to be sent him, which, as he has not yet come into

active operations, has probably been sufficient. My property is small—my income this year hardly up to my expenses; but to carry out the plan which Captain Brown
has matured, if the time seemed favorable, I would sacri-
fice both income and property, as he very well knows.
But it is probable that Captain Brown placed too much
confidence in the expectations of others, and that he may
have mistaken *hopes* for *promises.* Does he join in your
vituperation of his Boston friends? I know he does not.
I can excuse much to one who has so much reason for
anxiety as you have in the distress of your family."

Some things in this letter require explanation.
At this time, none of Brown's New England
friends, except possibly a few colored men at
Springfield, had any hint of his Virginia plans.
At the National Committee meeting of the
January previous, where Brown was, I represented
Drs. Cabot and Howe as their proxy, for the express purpose of having the National Committee
return our 200 rifles to the Massachusetts committee for Brown's use, to whom we had voted them.
The meeting did so return them, well knowing that
we should turn them over to Brown without delay.
He found them at Tabor in August or September,
and took possession, meaning then to use them in
Kansas, and not to sell them. It was with a part
of these rifles that he entered Virginia in October,
1859; but none of us knew in January, 1858, that
such a scheme was in contemplation.
At this Astor House meeting Brown was closely
questioned by some of the National Committee,

particularly by Mr. Hurd, of Chicago, as to what
he would do with money and arms. He refused to
pledge himself to use them solely in Kansas, and
declared that his past record ought to be a sufficient guarantee that he should employ them judi-
ciously. If we chose to trust him, well and good,
but he would neither make pledges nor disclose his
plans. Mr. Hurd had some inkling that Brown
would not confine his warfare to Kansas, but the
rest of us were willing to trust Brown, and the
money was voted.

It was probably Forbes's quarrel with Brown
that hastened his disclosure to us of the Virginia
plan, in the end of February, 1858, at Gerrit
Smith's house, after he had communicated it to
Frederick Douglass at Rochester. The latter had
heard something of the scheme at Springfield, in
1847. Of Forbes, Douglass says:

" After remaining with Brown a short time, he came to
me in Rochester (Nov., 1857) with a letter from him, asking me to receive and assist him. I was not favorably impressed with Forbes at first; but I ' conquered my preju-
dices,' took him to a hotel, and paid his board while he
remained. Just before leaving, he spoke of his family in
Europe as in destitute circumstances, and of his desire to
send them some money. I gave him a little, and through
Miss Ottilia Assing, a German lady deeply interested in
the John Brown scheme, he was introduced to several of
my German friends in New York. But he soon wore them
out by his endless begging; and when he could make no
more money by professing to advance the project, he
threatened to expose it and all connected with it. I was

the first to be informed of his tactics, and I promptly communicated them to Captain Brown. Through Miss Assing I found that Forbes had told Brown's designs to Horace Greeley, and to officials at Washington, of which I informed Brown; and this led to the postponement of the enterprise another year. It was hoped that by this delay the story of Forbes would be discredited; and this was correct—for nobody believed the scoundrel, though he told the truth."

I should scarcely use the word "scoundrel" of Forbes, although he did, now and then, the deeds of dishonor. Such was his vanity and his lack of self-control that what to men of honor seems unpardonable, must have appeared to Forbes quite in keeping with his lofty estimate of himself. We have seen not a few such instances, and often in persons much higher placed than this underbred Englishman. The "officials" whom he saw in Washington were anti-slavery Senators, and not members of the administration of Buchanan. Dr. Howe, writing to Senator Wilson in May, 1858, thus described Forbes:

" There is in Washington a disappointed and malicious man, working with all the activity which hate and revenge can inspire, to harm Brown, and to cast odium on the friends of Kansas in Massachusetts. You probably know him. He has been to Mr. Seward. Mr. (John P.) Hale also can tell you something about him."

To Forbes himself, Howe wrote thus, about the same time:

" I infer from your language that you have obtained (in confidence) some information respecting an expedition which you think to be commendable, provided *you* could manage it, but which you will *betray* and denounce if Brown does not give it up! You are, sir, the guardian of your own honor, but I trust that for your children's sake, at least, you will never let your passion lead you to a course that might make them blush."

Forbes himself, rather too late for his own reputation, seems to have taken the hint of Howe; for in October, 1859 (the 25th), he published in the New York *Herald,* to which he had made some disclosures, after Brown's arrest, this disclaimer:

" Some Abolitionists of good judgment insisted strongly that I should make Brown desist from his projects, which they considered would prove fatal to the anti-slavery cause; and as there were sundry persons in the free States interested, copies of most of the letters were furnished to each of them and to Brown. I could not myself take all the copies, therefore some friends occasionally copied for me. I feel sure that none of these letters were suffered to be seen by the Secretary of War: first, because I have faith in the reliability of those who had them in their hands; and, secondly, because it is absolutely impossible that, had such authentic evidence been placed before him, he could have been taken so by surprise as he was at Harper's Ferry."

Two days later, October 27, one A. Jones, for whom Governor Wise of Virginia vouched as " reliable," wrote to Wise, then investigating the Virginia Foray:

" It would be well for you to Telegraph to M^r. Hunter the prosecuting attorney at Charlestown to have Hugh Forbes, of this city, sumoned to that place as a witness. Here he is afraid of the abolitionists. I have no doubt, that he can make important disclosures if disposed, and, which would fully prove the Treasonable complicity of *Seward, Sumner & others*. If assured of perfect protection & safety in Va. I think he would disgorge. He is no doubt an abolition adventurer of a mean type, but, his disclosure might develope other & corroborative testimony, compromising *Seward* and his *confederates* in treason."

Soon after this date Forbes disappeared from New York, without "disgorging" anything that was not by that time pretty well known from other sources. His passage to Europe may have been paid from the money earned by his disclosures in the *Herald,* which was then struggling hard to connect Seward and Sumner with the plans of Brown. On the 28th of October it published editorially these remarks:

" The Forbes correspondence shows the connection of Seward with this vile conspiracy against the Union and the South. It appears from Colonel Forbes' correspondence that Mr. Seward was aware of this conspiracy as far back as the spring of 1858; he knew that an organized attempt would be made to create a servile insurrection, to overthrow the Union and plunge the country into blood, and it was with the full knowledge of this abominable scheme before him that he made his brutal speech at Rochester, declaring for an ' irrepressible conflict ' between the North and South. To verify his words, the sanguinary conflict opened the other day at Harper's Ferry, and had it not been prematurely commenced, and thus rapidly crushed, the sentiments enunciated at Rochester would have been transformed into deeds in Virginia and Maryland, the probable result of which may well startle the entire country."

But to return to the thread of my story. Being addressed by me and others to know what Forbes meant by his insulting letters in the early winter of 1857-8, Brown came eastward from Springdale, in Iowa, late in January, 1858, and early in February took refuge under the name of "Nelson Hawkins" with Douglass in Rochester, N. Y., paying him board for some weeks, at $3 a week. From there, February 2, he wrote to Theodore Parker, to whom I had introduced Brown thirteen months before, and said:

"I am again out of Kansas, and am at this time concealing my whereabouts; but for very different reasons, however, from those I had for doing so at Boston last spring. I have nearly perfected arrangements for carrying out an important measure in which the world has a deep interest, as well as Kansas; and only lack from five to eight hundred dollars to enable me to do so—the same object for which I asked for secret-service money last fall. It is my only errand here; and I have written to some of our mutual friends in regard to it, but they none of them understand my views so well as you do, and I cannot explain without their first committing themselves more than I know of their doing. I have heard that Parker Pillsbury and some others in your quarter hold out ideas similar to those on which I act; but I have no personal acquaintance with them, and know nothing of their

*Your Friend
John Brown*

(From the last Boston photograph, 1859)

influence or means. Cannot you either by direct or indirect action do something to further me? Do you not know of some parties whom you could induce to give their abolition theories a thoroughly practical shape? I hope this will prove to be the last time I shall be driven to harass a friend in such a way. Do you think any of my Garrisonian friends, either at Boston, Worcester, or any other place, can be induced to supply a little ' straw,' if I will absolutely make ' bricks'? I have written George L. Stearns, Esq., of Medford, and Mr. F. B. Sanborn, of Concord; but I am not informed as to how deeply-dyed Abolitionists those friends are, and must beg you to consider this communication strictly confidential—unless you know of parties who will feel and act, and hold their peace. I want to bring the thing about during the next sixty days."

This letter was shown to me, and I had received one of like tenor, as Higginson and Stearns had. At the same time one of our Kansas correspondents wrote me that Brown had disappeared from Kansas and Iowa, and that some thought him insane. This, combined with the intimations of Forbes, led me to imagine that Brown had some scheme for an uprising of the slaves—but if so, I supposed it might occur on the Kansas border, or in some inland part of Missouri. February 7 my classmate Morton wrote me from Mr. Smith's house, quoting the substance of Brown's letter to Smith. " He thinks he can do with the money more than all that has yet been done. He wishes to avoid publicity, and so does not come here, and will not see his family. This is news—he "expects to overthrow slavery in a large part of the country." Gerrit Smith invited Brown to his Peterboro house, and (February 19) Morton wrote me again:

" John Brown is here, and asks me to say to you he is waiting here to see you. If you cannot come within the time he named—say the middle of next week—let him know by letter enclosed to me, when you can come. He says 'tis not possible for him to go East, under the circumstances. He would very much like to see you."

The next day (February 20) Brown wrote to his son John thus:

" I am here with our good friends Gerrit Smith and wife, who, I am most happy to tell you, are ready to go in for a share in the whole trade. I will say (in the language of another), in regard to this most encouraging fact, ' My soul doth magnify the Lord.' I seem to be almost marvelously helped; and to His name be praise! I had to-day no particular thing to write, other than to let you share in my encouragement. . . . (Feb. 22) I have still need of all the help I can possibly get, but am greatly encouraged in asking for it. Mr. Smith thinks you might operate to more advantage in Nèw England, about Boston, than by going to Washington—say in the large country towns. I think he may be right. Do as you think best."

On the evening of this later date, the 22d, I reached Peterboro from Albany, where I had spent Sunday, and found Brown there, domesticated and enjoying the society of an old officer of Wellington's army in Spain, Captain Charles Stewart, who had met Brown there in June, 1855, and given $5 toward arming the Brown family in Kansas. Brown had been there since the preceding Thursday, and had unfolded much of his plans to the Smiths. After dinner, and after an hour spent with other guests in the parlor, I went with Mr. Smith, John Brown, and my classmate Morton, to the room of Mr. Morton in the third story. Here, in the long winter evening that followed, Brown unfolded for the first time to me his plans for a campaign somewhere in slave territory east of the Alleghanies. In an upper chamber of Gerrit Smith's villa at Peterboro, where, amid inherited acres which he managed with noble generosity, that baronial democrat lived and bore his part in our struggle for liberty, he unfolded them to me and my classmate Morton, of Plymouth; for he had already opened them to Mr. and Mrs. Smith, in more private conversations, and they had signified a general approval. Now he read us the singular constitution drawn up by him (in the Frederick Douglass house at Rochester) for the government of the territory, small or large, which he might rescue by force from slavery, and for the control of his own little band. It was an amazing proposition —desperate in its character, wholly inadequate in its provision of means, and of most uncertain result. Such as it was, Brown had set his heart on it as the shortest way to restore our slave-cursed republic to the principles of the Declaration of Independence; and he was ready to die in its execution—as he did.

To begin this hazardous adventure he asked for but eight hundred dollars, and would think himself rich with a thousand. Being questioned and opposed, he laid before us in detail his methods of organization and fortification; of settlement in the South, if that were possible, and of retreat through the North, if necessary; and his theory of the way in which such an invasion would be received in the country at large. He desired from his friends a patient hearing of his statements, a candid opinion concerning his plan, and, if that were favorable, then such aid in money and support as we could give him.

We listened until after midnight, proposing objections and raising difficulties; but nothing could shake the purpose of the old Puritan. Every difficulty had been foreseen and provided against in some manner; the grand difficulty of all—the manifest hopelessness of undertaking anything so vast with such slender means—was met with the text of Scripture: " If God be for us, who can be against us? " He had made nearly all his arrangements: he had so many men enlisted, so many hundred weapons; all he now wanted was the small sum of money. With that he would open his campaign in the spring, and he had no doubt that the enterprise " would *pay*," as he said.

We dissuaded him from what we thought certain failure; urging all the objections that would naturally occur to persons desiring the end he was seeking, but distrusting the slender means and the unpropitious time. But no argument could prevail

against his fixed purpose; he was determined to
make the attempt, with many or with few, and he
left us only the alternatives of betrayal, desertion
or support.

On the 23d of February the discussion was renewed, and, as usually happened when he had time
enough, Captain Brown began to prevail over the
objections. We saw we must either stand by him
or leave him to dash himself alone against the for-
tress he was determined to assault. To withhold
aid would only delay, not prevent him. As the sun
was setting over the snowy hills of the region where
we met, I walked for an hour with Gerrit Smith
among woods and fields (then included in his broad
manor) which his father purchased of the Indians
and bequeathed to him. Brown was left at home by
the fire, discussing points of theology with Charles
Stewart. Mr. Smith restated in his eloquent way
the daring propositions of Brown, whose import he
understood fully, and then said in substance: " You
see how it is; our dear old friend has made up his
mind to this course, and cannot be turned from it.
We cannot give him up to die alone; we must support him. I will raise so many hundred dollars for
him; you must lay the case before your friends in
Massachusetts, and ask them to do as much. I see
no other way." I had come to the same conclusion,
and by the same process of reasoning. It was done
far more from our regard for the man than from
hopes of immediate success. But the Lord knows
His own soldiers, and the far-reaching results of
Brown's action in Virginia are now well known of all

men.   He struck at American slavery the severest
blow it had ever received; and his tragic experi-
ment, though for a few months it seemed to have
failed, was a great hastening cause of that bloody
rebellion in which slavery perished.   Brown was
executed December 2, 1859; three years and thirty
days afterward President Lincoln issued the final
decree of emancipation; and in a few years from
the date of Brown's death, not a slave remained in
bondage, of the four millions for whose redemp-
tion he had died.   Seldom in human history have
such great effects so rapidly followed magnan-
imous deeds.

Brown was an instrument in the hands of Providence to uproot and destroy an evil institution
which had never appeared more boastful, more
flourishing or more permanent than when, only
eight years before final emancipation, Brown entered the broad domain of Kansas, which the slaveholders, by force and fraud, were holding as their
own.   "I shall not be forward to think him mistaken in his method," said Thoreau, "who quickest
succeeds to liberate the slave."   Can any method be
found that could have done that work quicker than
Brown's?   Within six years from his execution
there was not a slave held in bondage in the United
States; but for Brown's career it might have been
sixty years before we reached that result.   His
attack and its consequences showed both North and
South the gulf on whose brink they were standing.
The infuriated slave-masters made haste to break
up the Union, which they saw might ultimately de-

stroy their system. Put thus to the test, our millions of the North were not slow to say: "We choose union without slavery, even at the cost of indefinite bloodshed, to any further union with slavemasters and traitors." The ancient belief was again justified, that in battle that army must win in whose vanguard the first victim devoted himself to death. Led on by a foreordination he felt but did not understand, Brown gave his life for the cause destined to succeed.

Unlike that French marshal who "spent a long life carrying aid to the stronger side," Brown lent his good sword to that which seemed the weaker, but which had God for its reserve. He was one of those rare types, easily passing into the mythical, to which belonged David, the shepherd; Tell, the mountaineer; Wallace, the outlaw, and Hofer, the Tyrolese innkeeper. Born of the people, humble of rank and obscure in early life, these men (if men they all were) drew toward them the wrath of the powerful, the love of the multitude; they were hunted, prisoned, murdered—but every blow struck at them only made them dearer to the heart of the humble. By these, and not by coteries of scholars in their libraries, the fame of heroes is established. In heroes, faults are pardoned, crimes forgotten, exploits magnified—their life becomes a poem or a scripture—they enter on an enviable earthly immortality.

From Gerrit Smith's house, the day I departed for Boston, Brown wrote me one of those prophetic letters which so seldom flowed from his pen;

this I have cherished as the most complete evidence of my friendship and unison with him:

John Brown to F. B. Sanborn.
PETERBORO', N. Y., Feb. 24, 1858.

MY DEAR FRIEND,—Mr. Morton has taken the liberty of saying to me that you felt half inclined to make a common cause with me. I greatly rejoice at this; for I believe when you come to look at the ample field I labor in, and the rich harvest which not only this entire country but the whole world during the present and future generations may reap from its successful cultivation, you will feel that you are out of your element until you find you are in it, an entire unit. What an inconceivable amount of good you might so effect by your counsel, your example, your encouragement, your natural and acquired ability for active service! And then, how very little we can possibly lose! Certainly the cause is enough to *live* for, if not to —— for. I have only had this one opportunity, in a life of nearly sixty years; and could I be continued ten times as long again, I might not again have another equal opportunity. God has honored but comparatively a very small part of mankind with any possible chance for such mighty and soul-satisfying rewards. But, my dear friend, if you should make up your mind to do so, I trust it will be wholly from the promptings of your own spirit, after having thoroughly counted the cost. I would flatter no man into such a measure, if I could do it ever so easily.

I expect nothing but to "endure hardness"; but I expect to effect a mighty conquest, even though it be like the last victory of Samson. I felt for a number of years, in earlier life, a steady, strong desire to die; but since I saw any prospect of becoming a "reaper" in the great harvest, I have not only felt quite willing to live, but have enjoyed life much; and am now rather anxious to live for a few years more.

Your sincere friend,

JOHN BROWN.*

The money desired by Brown was soon raised and placed in his hands, or at his order, but, as has been inferred from what I have said about Forbes, his threatened disclosures led to a postponement. Brown had come to Boston early in March, 1858, had there met Parker, Howe, and Stearns, had communicated his plans to them with sufficient full-ness, but had named no place for "opening the mill," as he styled his desperate venture. Neither of the three heard Harper's Ferry mentioned; and although Brown had casually asked me, at the American House in Hanover Street (where he then lodged, under the name of I. Smith), what I should think of an attack on the arsenal at Har-per's Ferry, it did not give me the impression that he meant to begin there. I had supposed, and con-tinued so to think, that the opening would be made much farther from Richmond and Washington.

* This letter was received soon after my return to Concord. On my way through Boston I had communicated to Theodore Parker at his house in Exeter Place, the substance of Brown's plan; and upon receiving the letter I transmitted it to Parker. He retained it, so that it was out of my possession in October, 1859, when I destroyed most of the letters of Brown and others which could com-promise friends. Some time afterward my letters to Parker came back to me, and among them this epistle. That it did not draw me into the field as one of Brown's band was because the interests of other persons were then too much in my hands and in my thoughts to permit a change in my whole course of life.

On this point his daughter Anne, now Mrs. Adams, of Petrolia, Cal., wrote me in 1885:

" That Father had a number of plans (and of places selected) for commencing operations, is now quite evident from the testimony of different persons with whom he talked. Salmon tells Mother that he at one time talked strongly of Baton Rouge—planning to go there and make a beginning, and so work his way north. There were very few colored men with him, though he spent years in trying to enlist more. He made the acquaintance of all such that he could, both high and low, in the United States and in Canada. That was what first took him to North Elba. His first and main object in going to Kansas was to find men, and an opening or base on which to commence operations—or, as he said, ' to see if something would not turn up to his advantage.' Yet he had planned to go to Harper's Ferry before he or any of our family had gone to Kansas. He told me his plan the winter before they all went (1854-5). I was then but eleven years old. He said I was old enough to understand, and that he knew he could trust me. Afterward, when a school-girl at N. Elba, I remember having a queer feeling if the class in Geography would have to recite the lesson on Virginia. How hard it was for me to recite about Harper's Ferry! I felt as if I might in some way betray Father's ' plan,' as we always called it. Little did I then think he was training me for future usefulness there."

Brown had communicated his purpose to his older children as long before as 1838, as three of his sons have personally assured me. Nothing was said of it to me by the Adirondac family in 1857; but I have reason to surmise that Gerrit Smith had heard of an attack proposed at Harper's Ferry, at some time in 1858 or 1859. Be that as it may, it was not made known to the rest of us, either by him or by Frederick Douglass, who knew of it in the summer of '59, if not sooner. On this point Anne said, in 1885:

" There is a missing link that makes Father's movements late in September and early in October, '59, a mystery to most of even of his friends. I could, if I thought best, supply that link. I do not know how much Owen knows or would be willing to tell, if he were asked, why Father and John Kagi went to Philadelphia the last of September. Father told Watson, Oliver, Kagi and myself; whether he let any one else know, I have no present means of finding out."

She probably had in mind the occasion late in September, when certain colored citizens of Philadelphia, who seem to have been raising recruits for Brown, wrote this letter to Frederick Douglass, urging him to join personally in Brown's foray:

F. D., Esq.

DEAR SIR,—The undersigned feel it to be of the utmost importance that our class be properly represented in a convention to come off right away (near) Chambersburg, in this State. We think you are the man of all others to represent us; and we severally pledge ourselves that in case you will come right on we will see your family well provided for during your absence, or until your safe return to them. Answer to us and to John Henrie, Esq., Chambersburg, Penn., at once. We are ready to make you a remittance, if you go. We have now quite a num-

ber of good but not very intelligent representatives collected.   Some of our members are ready to go on with
you."

Apparently Douglass did not go to this "convention," and it is certain that Brown felt some
dissatisfaction with him on that account.   Mrs.
Adams added to her statement above quoted, "No
public use should be made of this information during the lifetime of the party who was to blame, or
who caused the trouble."   "It was God," she con-
cludes, "who thwarted their purposes and substi-
tuted His own."   There were promises of help
from colored men in the North, represented by
Douglass, who had long known Brown's general
scheme, by J. W. Loguen of Syracuse, and J. N.
Gloucester of Brooklyn.   Behind them were supposed to stand Gerrit Smith, and possibly Henry
Ward Beecher.   Whether such promises were seri-
ously made will perhaps never be known; they were
not taken much into account by the New England
friends of Brown, who provided him with the
funds and the arms for his adventure.

The threatened revelations of Hugh Forbes
found Brown at St. Catharine's, in Canada, organ-
izing his force under the provisions of his theoretic
Constitution.   He had explained his methods to
Douglass in 1847, as he did to me at Peterboro in
1858.   They were slightly changed from time to
time, but they always left an alternative—either
to encamp and fortify on slaveholding territory,
but in a mountainous region—or else to make up
parties of freed slaves and send or lead them to

freedom in some Northern State, or in Canada.
The organization made in Canada was but the
skeleton of a larger body, which these few who
bore the titles were to command; but Brown neither
expected nor desired a large force, nor did he propose any general insurrection. He thought the
slaves would come in, or be brought in with considerable alacrity, and his theoretical difficulty, in
which he wanted my aid, was how to control his
men. The practical difficulty, as the event proved,
was to bring the slaves in, and the choice of Harper's Ferry as the point of attack made what was
before desperate enough, now practically impossible. Brown's men saw this, and remonstrated;
so did Douglass when informed of the place, and
so should we all have done, had the place been seri-
ously suggested to us, as it certainly was not, unless
possibly to Mr. Smith.

The prospect of betrayal by Forbes seemed in
May so threatening that advantage was taken of
Gerrit Smith's approaching visit to Boston, to sum-
mon a meeting of the secret committee of six—
Howe, Parker, Smith, Stearns, Higginson and
Sanborn—at Mr. Smith's room in the Revere
House, May 24, 1858, to consider what ought to
be done by us. All were present but Higginson,
and Brown too was absent. Active correspondence
had preceded this meeting. Smith had written me,
May 7,* "It seems to me that, in these circum-

---

* This letter and several of the others mentioned, are now
thought to be in the Boston Public Library, where Higginson, who
had preserved them from destruction, has deposited them.

stances, Brown must go no further, and so I write him. I never was convinced of the wisdom of his scheme. But as things now stand it would be madness to attempt to execute it. Col. Forbes would make such an attempt a certain and most disastrous failure." I had already, after conferring with Howe and Stearns, written to Higginson (May 5), thus:

" It looks as if the project must, for the present, be deferred, for I find by reading Forbes's epistles to the Doctor that he knows the details of the plan, and even knows (what very few do) that the Doctor, Mr. Stearns, and myself are informed of it. How he got this knowledge is a mystery. He demands that Hawkins be dismissed as agent, and *himself* or some other be put in his place, threatening otherwise to make the business public. Theodore Parker and G. L. Stearns think the plan must be deferred till another year; the Doctor does not think so, and I am in doubt, inclining to the opinion of the two former."

Higginson did not take this view, but wrote to Parker, May 9:

" I regard any postponement as simply abandoning the project; for if we give it up now, at the command or threat of H. F., it will be the same next year. The only way is to circumvent the man somehow (if he cannot be restrained in his malice). When the thing is well started, who cares what he says? "

He soon after wrote more fully to Parker, giving many arguments against delay. Parker replied: "If you knew all we do about 'Colonel' Forbes, you would think differently."

When, about May 20, Mr. Stearns met Brown in or near New York, it was arranged that Brown should thenceforth hold the 200 rifles as the agent of Mr. Stearns (whose property they then had been for some time), and that the State Committee should be relieved of responsibility for them. When the secret committee met at the Revere House, May 24, it had already been decided to postpone the attack; the questions remaining were whether Brown should go to Kansas at once (where the old troubles were breaking out again), and assist Montgomery and others, as he soon did— and what sum of money should be raised for his future use. The five members who met that day were united in voting that he should go to Kansas at once. A week later (May 31, 1858), Brown was in Boston, and there met Higginson, who made a record of their conversation at the time. Brown, he says, "was full of regret at the Revere House decision—to postpone the attack till the spring of 1859, when Brown was to receive from the secret committee $2000 or more; he, meanwhile, to blind Forbes by going to Kansas." Higginson adds:

"On probing Brown, I found that he . . . considered delay very discouraging to his thirteen men, and to those in Canada. Impossible to begin in the autumn; and he would not lose a day [he finally said] if he had three hundred dollars; it would not cost twenty-five dollars apiece to get his men from Ohio, and that was all he needed. The knowledge that Forbes could give of his plans would be injurious, for he wished his opponents to underrate him; but still . . . the increased terror produced would perhaps counterbalance this, and it would not make much difference. If he had the means he would not lose a day."

He complained that some of his Eastern friends were not men of action; that they were intimidated, and magnified the obstacles. Still, it was essential that they should not think him reckless, he said; " and as they held the purse, he was powerless without them, having spent nearly everything received this campaign, on account of delay—a month at Chatham, etc." Higginson notes down a few days later that Dr. Howe told him Brown left Boston, June 3, with five hundred dollars in gold, and liberty to retain all the arms, and that "he went off in good spirits." He visited North Elba, Ohio, and Iowa, on his way to Kansas, and finally reached Lawrence, June 25, 1858.

Some question has been raised, mostly by persons who never gave money or sympathy to the cause of freedom in Kansas, as to the good faith of these six gentlemen in consenting to the use of Mr. Stearns's rifles anywhere but in Kansas, where, in fact, they were no longer needed. These critics have forgotten, or never knew, that we had personally given at least $20,000 to the cause in Kansas; had administered much larger funds without fee or reward, generally without even charging our traveling expenses to the commit-

tee's treasury, and had in this service devoted many
months' time. We could not doubt that we had a
good right to use our own money for the support
of a movement that aimed at the same general result, and which time has shown to have been even
more effective than the freeing of Kansas. Every
dollar contributed by others than ourselves for the
cause of Kansas was strictly used by us for that
cause; and why could we not use our own contribution as we saw fit?

The relation of the Kansas Committee of Massachusetts to the rifles they had bought in 1856 was
one thing; that of Mr. Stearns to these arms was
quite another thing in 1858. He had virtually
bought back the two hundred rifles from the committee, which, though never formally dissolved, and
still continuing at intervals to pass votes and write
letters in its executive committee, had long been
practically defunct, for the good reason that its
funds were exhausted. It had supplied the starv-
ing people of Kansas with wheat and clothing in
1857; and to do this had advanced money far beyond the amount raised in that year. I remember
this, because I had myself advanced two or three
hundred dollars at that time; but the principal advances were made by our chairman, whose liber-
ality where his heart was interested knew no
bounds. At the time when his Massachusetts
friends first heard of the Virginia plans of Brown,
and gave their reluctant approval, the rifles in
Brown's possession, though nominally belonging
to the Massachusetts Kansas Committee, were

pledged to Mr. Stearns, along with other property, for the reimbursement of his advances. I have forgotten how many thousand dollars he paid in this way, but the value of the arms was not enough to reimburse him; and it was agreed that he should not only have these, but should also be at liberty to reimburse himself out of the avails of promissory notes given by the Kansas farmers in payment for the wheat and other supplies which we sent in to the poor men. It was for this particular service that my advances were made, in joining with Dr. Howe and Mr. Stearns in paying our endorsements on a note of E. B. Whitman, cashed in Kansas for this supply of provisions or seed-wheat.

It was now agreed by the secret committee that Brown should not tell us his plans in detail, we being willing to trust him with our money, and wishing for no report of progress save by action. This common wish was thus pithily expressed by Mr. Smith, when he wrote me six weeks after Brown had left Boston:

PETERBORO', July 26, 1858.
MR. F. B. SANBORN.

MY DEAR SIR,—I have your letter of the 23d instant. I have great faith in the wisdom, integrity, and bravery of Captain Brown. For several years I have frequently given him money toward sustaining him in his contests with the slave-power. Whenever he shall embark in another of these contests I shall again stand ready to help him; and I will begin with giving him a hundred dollars. I do not wish to know Captain Brown's plans; I hope he will keep them to himself. Can you not visit us this summer? We shall be very glad to see you.

With great regard, your friend,

GERRIT SMITH.

In spite of this understanding, I could not avoid some knowledge of the movements and plans of Brown, since I was the chief medium of his correspondence, when he was not in personal communication with some of us by visits. His forcible emancipation of a dozen slaves in western Missouri, in December, 1858, and their safe removal to Windsor, in Canada, was well known, and caused a price of $3000 to be set on his head. Nevertheless, he moved freely about the Northern States, and soon showed himself publicly at the home of Gerrit Smith. My friend Morton, with whom I was in frequent correspondence, from 1853 to his death at Morges, in Switzerland, in 1900, wrote me thus from Peterboro in the next spring:

". Wednesday Evening, April 13, 1859.

"You must hear of Brown's meeting this afternoon— few in number, but the most interesting I perhaps ever saw. Mr. Smith spoke well; G. W. Putnam read a spirited poem; and Brown was exceedingly interesting, and once or twice so eloquent that Mr. Smith and some others wept. Some one asked him if he had not better apply himself in another direction, and reminded him of his imminent peril, and that his life could not be spared. His replies were swift and most impressively tremendous. A paper was handed about, with the name of Mr. Smith for four hundred dollars, to which others added. Mr. Smith,

in the most eloquent speech I ever heard from him, said:
' If I were asked to point out—I will say it in his presence
—to point out the man in all this world I think most truly
a Christian, I would point to John Brown.' I was once
doubtful in my own mind as to Captain Brown's course.
I now approve it heartily, having given my mind to it
more of late.

"April 18.—Brown left on Thursday the 14th, and
was to be at North Elba to-morrow, the 19th. Thence
he goes ' in a few days ' to you. [He actually reached
my house in Concord, Saturday, May 7, and spent half
his last birthday with me.] He says he must not be trifled
with, and shall hold Boston and New Haven to their
word. New Haven advises him to forfeit five hundred
dollars he has paid on a certain contract, and drop it.
He will not. From here he went in good spirits, and
appeared better than ever to us, barring an affection of
the right side of his head. I hope he will meet hearty
encouragement elsewhere. Mr. Smith gave him four hundred dollars, I twenty-five, and we took some ten dollars
at the little meeting."

For " New Haven " here read " Collinsville "—
the contract was for the pikes made in that Connecticut town.

Quite apart from the sympathy between one
descendant of the Pilgrim Fathers and another,
on the great subject of human freedom, music
was a tie between Brown and Morton; for both
were devotedly fond of it, and Morton was a com-
poser as well as a spirited performer on the piano,
and one of a large family of vocalists, whom I
often heard sing in chorus at their waterside cot-

tage in Plymouth. When I went to Peterboro in February, '58, to meet Brown at Gerrit Smith's, and hear his plans, Morton played us some fine pieces in the drawing-room after dinner. Among others was Schubert's "Serenade," then a favorite number; and I saw the old Puritan, who sang a good part himself, sit weeping at the air. It reminded me of the bedesman in Keats:

" Northward he turneth through a little door,
    And scarce three steps ere music's golden tongue
Flattered to tears this aged man and poor:
    But, no; already had his death-bell rung;
    The joys of all his life were said and sung."

I had been looking for Brown in Concord for some days when a little after noon of Saturday, May 7, he appeared at my door (the residence now of Miss Mary and Miss Flora White, not far from the Fitchburg railroad station) accompanied by his faithful henchman, Jeremiah Anderson, of Iowa, who was killed at Harper's Ferry. We gave notice through the churches, Sunday morning, of a meeting that evening, at which Brown spoke, and a few persons gave him money. From the Journal of Bronson Alcott, I quote passages written after the meeting:

" *Concord, May* 8, 1859. This evening I hear Captain Brown speak at the Town Hall on Kansas affairs, and the part taken by him in the late troubles there. He tells his story with surpassing simplicity and sense, impressing us all deeply by his courage and religious earnestness. Our best people listen to his words—Emerson, Thoreau, Judge Hoar, my wife; and some of them contribute something in aid of his plans without asking particulars, such confidence does he inspire in his integrity and abilities. He is Sanborn's guest, and stays for a day only. A young man named Anderson accompanies him. They go armed, I am told, and will defend themselves, if necessary. I believe they are now on their way to Connecticut and farther south; but the Captain leaves us much in the dark concerning his destination and designs for the coming months. Yet he does not conceal his hatred of slavery, nor his readiness to strike a blow for freedom at the proper moment. I think him equal to anything he dares —the man to do the deed, if it must be done, and with the martyr's temper and purpose. He is of imposing appearance, personally,—tall, with square shoulders; eyes of deep gray, and couchant, as if ready to spring at the least rustling, dauntless yet kindly; his hair shooting backward from low down on his forehead; nose trenchant and Romanesque; set lips, his voice suppressed yet metallic, suggesting deep reserve; decided mouth; the countenance and frame charged with power throughout. Since here last he has added a flowing beard, which gives to the soldierly air the port of an apostle. Though sixty years old, he is agile, and ready for any audacity, in any crisis. I think him about the manliest man I have ever seen—the type and synonym of the Just."

Brown told the story of his invasion of Missouri, and the removal of the slaves; and there were good citizens and anti-slavery men in the audience who were startled at this practical enforcement of the Golden Rule, as Dr. Howe was, a few days later, when he met Brown in Boston.

The conversation was reported by Howe in a letter to Parker at Rome, the next winter. Writing to me from Peterboro, June 1, Morton said: "I suppose you know the place where this matter is to be adjudicated. Harriet Tubman suggested the 4th of July as a good time to 'raise the mill.'" I did not know the place, but Harriet was an old friend of mine—a Maryland Sibyl who had not only escaped from slavery herself, but had brought away a hundred other fugitives. She was intimate with the Smiths, with the Sedgwicks, of Syracuse, and the Sewards, of Auburn. In fact, it was on the anniversary of our national independence that Brown appeared in Maryland, on his way to the Kennedy Farm; but my only knowledge for months was of Chambersburg, where he received his recruits and supplies. A few days after this note of Morton's, quoting Harriet, Mr. Smith himself wrote to Brown at an Ohio address which I had sent him. This letter was captured at the Kennedy Farm, but so misprinted in the newspapers that its puzzling character became still more misleading. Correctly printed, it is as follows:

"PETERBORO', June 4, 1859.

"CAPTAIN JOHN BROWN.

"MY DEAR FRIEND,—I wrote you a week ago, directing my letter to the care of Mr. Stearns. He replied, informing me that he had forwarded it to Westport; but as Mr. Morton received last evening a letter from Mr. Sanborn, saying your address would be your son's home—namely, West Andover—I therefore write you without delay, and direct your letter to your son. I have done what I could thus far for Kansas, and what I could to keep you at your Kansas work. Losses by indorsement and otherwise have brought me under heavy embarrassment the last two years, but I must, nevertheless, continue to do, in order to keep you at your Kansas work. I send you herewith my draft for two hundred dollars. Let me hear from you on the receipt of this letter. You live in our hearts, and our prayer to God is that you may have strength to continue in your Kansas work. My wife joins me in affectionate regard to you, dear John, whom we both hold in very high esteem. I suppose you put the Whitman note into Mr. Stearns's hands. It will be a great shame if Mr. Whitman does not pay it. What a noble man is Mr. Stearns! How liberally he has contributed to keep you in your Kansas work!"

To such as could read between the lines, this was a disclosure of the whole method of the secret committee. No one of them might know at any given time where Brown was, but some other of the four persons named in the letter would be likely to know—George L. Stearns, Edwin Morton, F. B. Sanborn, and Mr. Smith himself. The phrase "Kansas work" misled none of these persons, who all knew that Brown had finally left Kansas and was to operate henceforth in the slave States. The hundred dollars given by Mr. Smith April 14, added to the two hundred named in this letter, and the note of E. B. Whitman, of Kansas, which Brown received from Mr. Smith, make up five hundred and eighty-five dollars, or more than one-fifth of the two thousand dollars which he told Brown he would help his "Eastern friends" raise.

Those friends were Stearns, Howe, Higginson, and Sanborn—for Parker was then in Europe, and unable to contribute.

About the date of this letter (June 4, 1859), there was a departure from Boston by Brown, of which I thus wrote to Higginson:

" Brown left Boston for Springfield and New York on Wednesday morning at 8.30, and Mr. Stearns has probably gone to New York to-day, to make final arrangements for him. Brown means to be on the ground as soon as he can, perhaps so as to begin by the 4th of July. He could not say where he should be for a few weeks, but letters are addressed to him, under cover to his son John, Jr., at West Andover, Ohio. This point is not far from where Brown will begin, and his son will communicate with him. Two of his sons will go with him. He is desirous of getting some one to go to Canada, and collect recruits for him among the fugitives—with Harriet Tubman or alone, as the case may be."

CHAPTER VI

Brown at the Kennedy Farm

IT is quite impossible to say how much money was received and expended by Brown in the two years (1858-9) when he was actively providing for his foray in Virginia; but seldom have such momentous results been produced with less outlay. Most of the smaller sums received by him went through my hands, while the larger amounts were paid to him directly by Mr. Stearns and other contributors. His secret committee kept no records, and its members mostly destroyed their letters to each other, after his capture, so that nobody need be injured by what had been written. But a small part of the correspondence was captured at the Kennedy Farm, for Brown had left most of his letters at North Elba.

Mrs. Gerrit Smith wrote to me in January, 1874, what I had heard from her son-in-law, Charles Miller, in November, 1859: "Immediately after the Harper's Ferry affair Mr. Smith destroyed all the letters touching Brown's movements which he had received from persons in any degree privy to those movements; and he took it for granted that his own similar letters to others had been destroyed." In replying (Jan. 16, 1874), I said:

"My first proceeding upon hearing of the attack at

Harper's Ferry, was to go over carefully all the papers and letters then in my hands, and destroy all that could implicate Mr. Smith or other persons. Two months later, when John A. Andrew placed in my hands my own letters to Brown (with a few from other persons), which Mr. Phillips had brought down from North Elba, after the funeral there, I went over these also carefully, before I left Boston that day, and destroyed what would implicate others. But some of the correspondence of 1858-59 had lodged with Theodore Parker, and came back to me a year or two after his death; this I did not destroy. Colonel Higginson also had retained some of the letters which passed through my hands, with copies of many that he wrote to me or to Brown, and all these still exist. It is likely Mrs. Stearns has documents touching the matter. I should doubt if Dr. Howe had many; but Vice-President Wilson told me, some weeks ago, that he had recovered an important letter of his own, which in 1859-60 was supposed to be lost, when it went to Canada or somewhere, but has now got home again. It cannot, therefore, be assumed that all written evidence in the case is lost."

In fact, I have since found several of the notes which passed between members of the secret committee. I have accounts of $750 given by Smith to Brown in 1859; Mr. Stearns in that year gave him more than $1000; and Francis Merriam gave him $600 in gold. Out of a little more than $4000 paid by the secret committee, or by them known to be contributed in aid of the Virginia enterprise, at least $3800 was given with a clear knowledge of the use to which it would be put; while the rest was given by persons who were willing to trust

Brown without asking questions. It was Brown's custom to write one letter to be read by the half-dozen persons, outside of his own family, with whom he communicated. This letter commonly came to me first; and my custom was to show it to Mr. Parker and Dr. Howe, when they were at home, then to send it to Mr. Stearns, who sometimes forwarded it to Higginson or some more distant correspondent, and sometimes returned it to me.

Of the small band who went to their fate in Virginia with Brown, Colonel Hinton and Dr. Thomas Featherstonhaugh have collected and published many facts and anecdotes. But I have received, from Anne Brown Adams and others, pithy or pathetic incidents and traits, that are worth preserving. I knew personally nearly half of them, either before or after the tragedy. Anne Brown herself, with her sister-in-law, Martha Brewster, the young wife of Oliver Brown, went from the Adirondac woods to the Kennedy Farm in July, '59, to " keep house " for the party, and Anne has written me this:

" Of all the helpers Father had, none did their work better or more faithfully than poor, patient Martha Brewster, Oliver's wife. Whatever her hand found to do, she did it with her might. ' Oh, why did they not leave the Ferry sooner? '—this was the tearless cry that came like a dry sob from her lips *so* constantly. I never heard her utter one word of complaint at her hard lot,—only that pitiful cry. I never saw her shed a tear but once. When I held her dead baby for her to take a last look,

two scalding tears dropt on the little face as she bent over
and kissed it. I believe they were the only tears that
ever relieved her breaking heart; for she surely died of
a broken heart—she had no disease. She told me one
night before the baby was born, ' If I have a child that
lives, then I am going to try to live and raise it; but if
that dies, I am going to die too.' I said, ' Mat, you must
not die—we cannot spare you.' She said, ' If my child
dies I shall not have any object to live for; why should
you wish me to live then? ' "

She died at Mrs. Brown's house in the winter
following the tragedy at Harper's Ferry, and I
was in the house spending the night when her child
died. She was a fair and gentle person, quite jus-
tifying what Anne says of her, who thus continues:

" She died in March, 1860, and had she lived till April
she would have been married but two years. Married at
fifteen, she died when she was but seventeen years old; she
was a wife, mother and childless widow in less than two
years. Her little Olive died in February, less than three
days old. When Oliver married her in 1858, he expected
to go right away with Father; and as her parents were
bitterly opposed to ours, he thought the world would
allow his wife a shelter with us. That was their reason
for marrying so young. She was dignified and womanly
beyond her years. William Thompson (killed at the
Ferry) used to call her ' Mom's Lady '; the reason was,
he told me, that the first time he ever saw her, a small,
fair-haired child, on the fence with her sisters, as he was
going by the house—he asked their names. The others
told theirs, but she kept still until he asked again, when
she replied, ' Oh, I am Mom's Lady.' He said, as he told

the story, ' She is Mom's Lady still.' She seldom made a joke; life seemed too serious to her.

" Martha received a letter from Oliver late in June, and early in July we set forth for the Kennedy Farm. In coming downstairs, the morning we started, Martha sprained her ankle, and fainted with the pain. Every one said we would have to wait a few days; but she said, ' No, we will go all the same.' The occasion of our going was that Father found he would be obliged to have house-keepers, to ward off suspicion, after he rented the Farm; so he sent Oliver back for us. When we reached the hotel at Harper's Ferry, it was a little before dinner, and Father had just gone with a load of things up to the Farm, five miles off. So, after dinner, Oliver footed it up there, and Father came back after us about sundown.

" Our nearest neighbors were a family who had rented the garden that was just behind our house—so they had a good excuse for coming at all times to look at the garden—and at us. Little Mother Huffmaster and her brood of three little girls (the oldest seven years old) and a big boy baby—all barefooted, little Mother and all —had a troublesome way of calling on us at all hours of the day. Sometimes she would appear when the men— ' Invisibles,' I called them—were downstairs at their meals. I would tell them, shut the door, and stand on the porch to keep her out as long as I could, finding some excuse; while Martha would put things out of sight, in the kitchen, and the men would all go upstairs again—taking the victuals, dishes, table-cloth and all with them. This would all be done without so much noise as the rattling of a spoon. It happened quite frequently; but we did not dare to offend her, however troublesome, for fear she would tell what she saw. So I would give her things, to keep her friendly.

"One day, as I was clearing away the dinner, I drew a long sigh. Father said, 'What is the matter, Annie? Are you homesick?' With my usual lack of tact and good sense I blurted out, 'Yes—homesick and sick of living this life, where I have to live a lie—going by another name, and telling so many lies—or, what is the same, acting them. I wish you would hurry and get through with me, and let me go home, where I can be myself and have my own name again.' Father dropt his head, and a pained look came over his face; when Whipple (Stevens), who could always think of the right thing to say or do, at the right time and place, came to the rescue by saying, 'Annie, let me give you a piece of advice: Always tell the truth, the whole truth, and nothing but the truth; but if ever you *do* have to tell a lie, tell a whopper.' The laugh that followed this took the sting out of my hateful speech, and put all of us in good humor.

"I am glad to say that I did not often indulge myself in making remarks so painful as this must have been to my Father. He use to encourage us to argue and discuss questions with him, either to amuse himself or to find out our opinions on certain subjects. One day he and Oliver were discussing the Woman Question—Oliver contending that women generally were not so intelligent and smart as men. Father replied, 'I think my girls are quite as smart and intelligent as my boys. Ruth can write a letter quite as good, and perhaps better, than any of her brothers; and Anne here succeeds quite well in holding her own in a dispute with any of you boys.' As disputing was my ruling passion, all agreed, with a laugh at my expense that settled the question.

"In our housekeeping Martha divided the work, giving me what she thought I could do best. As she prided herself on being one year older, and for that reason having had more experience, she reserved some of the particularly nice work, like ironing fine shirts and making light bread, for herself to do. Once when I told her that, on account of the boys helping me with the dishes and the coarse ironing (which was my part), I did not think I was doing my share; and if she would teach me how, I offered to help iron the fine shirts and make bread. 'No,' she said, 'I would rather iron them myself. As for the light bread—you can make better corn-bread and Father's shortcakes (he taught me how to make those) than I can; but I seem to succeed better with the light bread than you. So we will each make our own kind. I never will attempt to make the shortcake—and if you helped on the bread, then you would be doing more than your share.'

"One day Father came home from a neighbor's where he had performed some kind of a surgical operation (lanced a wen on the neck of a woman, I think); the people gave him a dog. He was either a mixture of all breeds, or else of no breed at all—the ugliest brute I ever saw. I called out, as he came leading it into the yard, 'Oh, what *are* you going to do with that horrid dog?' 'Why, I thought we needed a dog to bark nights, if any one came here and wanted to get in; and I meant to get one anyway.' I said, 'Can't you carry out your "Plan" (we always spoke of the intended attack as "Father's Plan") without the help of that miserable, ugly pup?' He laughed and said, 'No, I do not think I can,' while he tied the dog in the smoke-house. He then told me that the boy who gave it to him said his name was 'Cuffee'; and he hoped I would not let my prejudice against it make me unkind, 'for you don't know what a good dog he may turn out to be.' Presently it howled dismally at being tied up, and I called out, 'Father, your baby is crying.' Then he told me he wished I would take something down to him and feed him, and so make friends with Cuffee. I confess I felt a repugnance towards the ugly pup; but it afterward repaid me by its strong attachment and doggish love, for all the kindness I ever bestowed on it.

"I am not telling these little stories because I thought they had any bearing in particular on the work that was to follow; but only to convince those who believe that John Brown was a crazy fanatic, stern and revengeful, and his followers a set of cutthroats and land-pirates, or wild adventurers, at least. They were, instead, a good-natured, mild-mannered set of men, with hearts tender and gentle as a woman's—believing in the Golden Rule, taking that for a text, and preaching a practical sermon to the world. They spent their time, while shut up in the house, in reading, singing, playing games, telling stories and helping Martha and me about the work. In their fun and play they were as innocent and as easily pleased as a lot of children; but when the great trial of strength came, we found them all brave and unflinching.

"I see that Owen has told you of the trouble and dissatisfaction among the men, and about Kagi's coming down from Chambersburg to help settle it. After breakfast that morning Father told me to leave my work until after the wagon started back to Chambersburg, and to stay on the porch ' on guard '; for the men had all gone upstairs. After a while Kagi came down into the dining-room and said, ' He had to wait a few minutes for Watson to get ready, and would like, if I had no objection, to sit down there and talk with me.' I told him he might, if he would keep in the dining-room far enough to be out of sight, and would run if I told him; that I was on guard, and had strict orders not to let him be seen. He made some remark about its being very odd for so young a girl to be standing guard, in such a place and for such a purpose.

" I told him that was my business nearly all the time. When I had to go in the kitchen to help Martha, then some of the men watched. He seemed quite surprised when he found that I understood all Father's plans. Among other things I remember asking him what he thought of Fred Douglass's refusal to come down with us. He said he did not blame Douglass, for ' he is physically incapable of running '; that he had some disease in his feet and limbs that made it impossible for him to run. ' If he had always lived on such plain food as you have here, he would be in a better condition to go. Besides, if Douglass were caught it would be sure death to him, for he had been a slave in Maryland.'

" Kagi did not seem to take a thought of the risk he was running in coming down among us. His relatives all lived near Harper's Ferry; he was raised thereabout, and whenever he went home on a visit he used to ' run off ' a slave or two belonging to his relatives, until he had helped away five or six. Then his friends informed him that if he ever came back again, they would lynch him. In proof of this fact Oliver told me this story:

" When, about July 4th, Father, Kagi, Anderson, Owen and Oliver first went down to the Ferry, they stopped at a little place called Sandy Hook, not far from the Ferry. There part of them boarded until after Oliver came back with Martha and me. One day Oliver and Kagi were sitting outside the hotel there, talking. A man coming along asked Oliver to take a turn with him, and then inquired if he knew the man he was talking with. Oliver said ' No '—he was a stranger who had got off the cars and was talking to him. ' Well,' said the man, ' he looks like John Kagi, and I believe it is he.' Oliver told Kagi as soon as he could get a chance unobserved, and it was decided that he had better go back at once to Chambersburg. Kagi was a tall, fine-looking man, pleasant and gentlemanly in his manners; and yet as earnest and enthusiastic in the ' cause ' as Father himself was. I never saw him but that once, and afterward, when we met in the Harrisburg depot, and I bade him and Father good-bye. He had a remarkable memory. When a boy he would commit from three to five hundred verses of the Bible in an incredibly short time, and repeat them at Sabbathschool—receiving prizes for so doing. He could read several pages of a book over twice, close the book, and at once repeat them almost word for word. He also wrote a fine clerkly hand.

" My association with the men at Kennedy Farm was necessarily very intimate, as I had the entire charge of the dining-room, and the stairway came down into that room, where they were allowed to come whenever we did not have company—which we seldom had. I waited upon them, watched and cared for them; and I must say that they would compare favorably with men in any station of life that I have ever met. They did not impress me as ' men who could do bloody deeds—the bloodier the better,' as was said at a public meeting; but as men who were earnest and true, kind and generous, warm-hearted and sympathetic; neither saints nor the worst of sinners. They nearly all seemed to be impressed with the idea that they were going to their death; one, Stewart Taylor, described his death to me. He was a very peculiar person, a firm believer in Spiritualism; so was Stevens also; but their belief was more in theory than in practice. One who escaped told me of their march down to Harper's Ferry, on the night of October 16. They went along an old, deserted road on the top of the mountain. He said ' they

all felt like they were marching to their own funeral.'
But still not a man faltered, though most of them had left
near and dear friends to go down there. I am often asked
why they did this? I can only say, They loved their country better than themselves. Their only success lies in the
effect produced on the American people, who were thus
prepared for what was so soon to follow."

Of the twenty-two men who actually composed
Brown's company at the Kennedy Farm (for
John Anderson, a colored recruit, never reached
there), I met ten, first and last, and Anne Brown
was in 1860 a pupil of mine at Concord. What
she says of them is no exaggeration; they were
mostly young men of excellent principles and gentle character, and several of them of much ability
and promise. Of the two Andersons, J. G. (a Wisconsin man by birth, but a resident afterward of
Iowa and Kansas), was once a guest of mine; the
other, a dark mulatto, Osborne P. Anderson, came
to see me in Boston long after the foray, in 1872,
shortly before his death. Of him Mrs. Adams
says:

" Did you know of the shameful way the majority of
the colored people treated Osborne Anderson, the only
colored man who escaped? He told me with tears in his
eyes and voice that, while escaping through Pennsylvania,
his own father turned him from the door, threatening to
have him arrested if he ever came again; and that most
of the colored people he met turned the cold shoulder to
him as if he was an outcast. Dangerfield Newby, except
Green, the only other colored man I knew (for Coleman

and Leary went down after I came away) was the son of
a Scotchman, and was born and raised not far from the
Ferry. His father took the mother and children to Ohio
and liberated them. Newby seemed a good-natured, sensible old man. He had a wife and several children that
were slaves, and he was impatient to have operations commenced, for he was anxious to get them. Green was a
perfect rattlebrain in talk; he used to annoy me very
much, coming downstairs so often. He came near betray-
ing and upsetting the whole business, by his careless let-
ting a neighbor woman see him, when she came to the
house one day. I had to do a great deal of talking and
some bribing to hush her up.

"The idea of capturing Col. Lewis Washington and
the General Washington arms originated with John E.
Cook. Poor man! it is best to cover his sins with the
mantle of charity. Perhaps we may say of him what I
used to hear Brother Watson say of any one whom he
heard accused of wrong motives—'Oh, probably he meant
well, but had a poor way of showing it.' There was an
old song called 'Faded Flowers,' a great favorite with
Tidd and Stevens, which they used to sing almost every
day at Kennedy Farm. Tidd sang the air, and Stevens
a peculiarly fine, soft bass. He was a bugler in the army
during the Mexican War; and I heard Father say one
day, after listening to him singing upstairs, 'He must
have caught those notes from his bugle.' 'Nearer My
God to Thee' was also often sung; and still another song
was,

'I know that the angels are whispering to thee.'

One of their songs I tried in vain to find years afterward,
or to hear of somebody who had ever heard it; but when
I read Scott's 'Lady of the Lake' I discovered it—the

boat-song of triumph chanted by the clansmen of Roderick Dhu:

' Hail to the Chief who in triumph advances!
     Honored and blest be the evergreen Pine!
Long may the tree in his banner that glances
     Flourish, the shelter and grace of our line!' "

The contrast between the triumph of the Highlanders and the failure of the foray of Brown and his men must have been pathetic to poor Anne and her bereaved kindred in the pine forest of the Adirondacs. She goes on:

" The night before we started from Kennedy Farm for North Elba, they sang ' Home Again ' for us. We left on the morning of September 29. Watson took Oliver, Martha and me in the little wagon up to Chambersburg. Oliver came on as far as Troy, N. Y., where we stayed over Sunday. Monday morning he put us on the train for Whitehall, and then he started back to Kennedy Farm —and death. Watson waited at Chambersburg for Father and Kagi, whom we met while changing cars in the Harrisburg depot; they were returning from Philadelphia. Father had planned that we should meet there, and told Watson, when he sent him down after us, that if nothing happened to prevent, we would all meet there. It was the last time I ever saw Father. I never looked at him after he was brought home; preferred to remember him just as we parted.

" While we were on the road to Chambersburg, driving along the great Turnpike on the way to Hagerstown, a man rode rapidly towards us from another road, as if he had been waiting for the wagon to appear—at least we thought so, and that he might be a 'patrol.' He passed by, and then, wheeling around, came up with Watson, who was then riding behind us. They had a horse and a mule, and took turns riding and driving—changing the animals on the road. The man rode alongside of Watson for some distance, asking all manner of questions about his business. He said, 'What do you carry in there?' drawing the cover aside and looking into the back of the wagon. Watson replied, 'I have two girls in there now.' The man made a polite bow, and said, 'Excuse me, ladies, —I did not know you were in there.' He then repeated his question, 'What do you carry in that wagon?—you drive by here so often—is it wool?' To this last abrupt question, Watson, for want of a better answer, said 'Yes.' He soon left us, going off as he came, on a side road. We were alarmed for fear of being arrested; but nothing came of it. When the man was out of sight Watson said, 'I guess he would have been surprised if he had found out that all the wool I ever carried in this wagon was on the heads of negroes.' He meant that the colored recruits were so brought down from Chambersburg by night."

Commenting on Dr. Howe's conversation with John Brown in the summer of 1859, censuring him for taking the horses and other property of the Missouri slaveholders, whose human property he carried away to freedom in Canada, Mrs. Adams writes me:

" It was after Father had become weary and even dis-couraged with begging for money and men to carry out his Plan, that he made up his mind to confiscate property that the slave or his ancestors had been compelled to earn for others—property that he needed to subsist on, and to enable him to free himself and others. He would have scorned even the idea of making any other personal use of such property than while he was engaged in working in their behalf. Dr. Howe and Father were both right— only they viewed the situation from different points. At a former time, when Dr. Howe was parting from Father, he gave him a little walnut box with a fine Smith & Wesson revolver in it. Father gave me the box, and I have it still. Now in this gift, Dr. Howe fully expected Captain Brown to break the law against carrying concealed weapons— and possibly the Commandment, ' Thou shalt not kill '—if he was attacked."

It was before the return of the young house-keepers to North Elba that the scene occurred be-tween Brown and his men, when they protested against going to their death in an attack on Harper's Ferry. Owen Brown, with whom I have talked whole days at his island retreat in Lake Erie, before he migrated to California, gave me this statement concerning that matter. Owen's memory was as wonderfully exact as that of any person I have known, and when he repeated any anecdote, I always found it was in the same form. He said:

" In the early part of September Father and I went with the horse and wagon from the Kennedy Farm to Chambersburg—and at different times after in September and October—to see if any *express packages* (colored vol-unteers) had arrived. We had many earnest discussions as to the feasibility of making the attack at Harper's Ferry—which plan was not known to any of us until after our arrival at the Kennedy Farm. All of our men, except Merriam, Kagi, Shields Green, and the colored men (the latter knowing nothing of Harper's Ferry), were opposed to striking the first blow there. During our talk on the road, I said to Father: 'You know how it resulted with Napoleon when he rejected advice in regard to marching with his army to Moscow. I believe that in your anxiety to see that all is going on well at the three different points proposed to be taken (the Arsenal, the Rifle-works, and the Magazine), you will so expose yourself as to lose your life.' He said, finally, 'I feel so depressed on account of the opposition of the men, that at times I am almost willing to temporarily abandon the undertaking.' I replied, 'We have gone too far for that—we must go ahead.' In the course of our talk he said to me, as he had many times to his men before, 'We have here only one life to live, and once to die; and if we lose our lives it will perhaps do more for the cause than our lives could be worth in any other way.' As we found no *express packages* at Chambersburg, he remained there with Kagi, and I went back alone. In a day or two both returned to the Kennedy Farm; the next morning he called all his men together in the chamber of the house, and said to them, 'I am not so strenuous about carrying out any of my particular plans as to do knowingly that which might probably result in an injury to the cause for which we are struggling;' and he repeated what he had said to me about our losing our lives. He then added, 'As you are all opposed to the plan of attacking here, I will resign; we will choose another leader, and I will faithfully obey, reserving to myself the privilege of giving counsel and advice where I think a better course could be adopted.' He did then resign. I first replied that I did not know of any one to choose as a leader in preference to him.

In a short time, probably within five minutes, he was again chosen as the leader."

Some of the company afterward became reconciled to the desperate attack; but most of them, as they marched down the misty mountain road from the Farm to the Ferry, felt that they were going to their death. Not so Jeremiah Anderson, who wrote to his Iowa brother, late in September, in a confident tone, and with expressions which show that no large force of the liberators was expected. The original date for the attack was fixed for about October 25; but it was hastened from local suspicions that the nature of the party at the Farm was other than it seemed. Anderson wrote:

" Our mining company will consist of between twenty-five and thirty, well equipped with tools. You can tell Uncle Dan it will be impossible for me to visit him before next spring. If my life is spared, I will be tired of work by that time, and I shall visit my relatives and friends in Iowa, if I can get leave of absence. At present, I am bound by all that is honorable to continue in the course. We go in to win, at all hazards. So if you should hear of a failure, it will be after a desperate struggle, and loss of capital on both sides. But that is the last of our thoughts. Everything seems to work to our hands, and victory will surely perch upon our banner. The old man has had this operation in view for twenty years; and last winter was just a hint and trial of what could be done. I expect (when I start again traveling) to start at this place and go through the State of Virginia, and on south,

just as circumstances require; mining and prospecting,
and carrying the ore with us."

For half a day Brown and his seventeen men—
five being left as guards on the Maryland side of
the Potomac—held the little town at the Ferry,
with its important government arsenal, at his
mercy, and had several captured hostages for prisoners. He and his band might then, possibly, have
escaped, and, by virtue of the alarm they excited,
might have retired in comparative safety. But for
some reason never fully explained, Brown lingered till escape was impossible; and it was the
design and expectation of those who captured him
in the little engine-house, to kill him on the bloody
floor, to which a lieutenant of marines struck him
down, and continued to wound him after he fell.
Heaven had other designs, and he survived to hold
a historic colloquy with the enraged Virginians,
which converted millions to Brown's cause, and de-
prived the victors of the fruit of their success.
His trial and execution added to the effect of his
words, and his letters from the Charlestown prison
completed his *Apologia pro vita sua.* On this I
will not dwell; his biographies are numbered by
tens, and his career gave world-wide vogue to a
war-song in the long contest that ensued. It soon
became evident to the world that his fate was just
that which he had anticipated in his letter to me of
February 24, 1858: "*I expect nothing but to endure hardness; but I expect to effect a mighty*

conquest, even though it be like the last victory of Samson."

                    Samson hath quit himself
Like Samson, and heroically hath finished
A life heroic; honor hath left, and freedom,—
And, which is best and happiest yet, all this
With God not parted from him, as was feared,
But favoring and assisting to the end.
Nothing is here for tears, nothing to wail
Or knock the breast,—no weakness, no contempt,
Dispraise or blame; nothing but well and fair,
And what may quiet us in a death so noble.

Wotton, Henry

How happy is he born & taught
That serveth not another's will;
Whose armour is his honest thought,
And simple truth his utmost skill:

Whose passions not his masters are,
Whose soul is still prepared for death,
Not tied unto the world with care
Of princes' ear, or vulgar breath.

Whose state can neither ... ...tions feel

Nor ruin make oppressors great.

Who envies none whom chance doth raise,
Or vice: Who never understood
How deepest wounds are given with praise;
Nor rules of state, but rules of good;

This man is freed from servile bands
Of hope to rise, or fear to fall:
Lord of himself, though not of lands;
And having nothing, yet hath all. Wotton

EMERSON'S AUTOGRAPH (TWO LINES) THEN THOREAU'S. 1859

CHAPTER VII

The Harper's Ferry Alarm

THE attack on Harper's Ferry by John Brown and his seventeen men, October 16, 1859, and his subsequent capture by the United States marines under Colonel Robert Lee (afterward the Confederate general-in-chief), were telegraphed to a startled world the next day or two, and reached me in my quiet schoolrooms at Concord on Tuesday morning. Arrangements had been made for the annual chestnutting excursion of my pupils and others, to the Estabrook woods on the old Carlisle road, for the whole day of Thursday. The interval gave me the information that an indefinite number of my letters, with those of Gerrit Smith, Dr. Howe, and others, had been captured at the Kennedy Farm; and nobody knew to what extent the records of our conspiracy were in the hands of the slaveholding authorities, headed by Senator Mason and Governor Wise. Time was also given me to decide what course immediately to take, and to consult with Mr. Stearns, Dr. Howe and Wendell Phillips. I therefore spent hours, Tuesday and Wednesday nights, searching my papers to destroy such as might compromise other persons; and on Thursday morning, after sending the pupils under competent teachers to the picnic, I took a chaise and drove across the country to the villa of Mr. Stearns in Medford. With him in my company I drove into Boston to consult John A. Andrew, an eminent counsel, well known to Stearns, Phillips and myself, as to the proper course to be taken, if we were liable to arrest in Massachusetts, either as witnesses or conspirators. Threats of that sort began to be made in the pro-slavery newspapers of New York, particularly the *Herald,* then commonly known as "the Satanic Press"; and we put our case before our friend Andrew, without stating to him the full particulars of our complicity with Brown. It being the opinion of Mr. Andrew, as expressed on Thursday, October 20, that we might be suddenly and secretly arrested and hurried out of the protection of Massachusetts law; and it seeming to me very important that the really small extent of our movement should be concealed, and its reach and character exaggerated, I went to Boston prepared to go that night on the route through Maine to Canada. After leaving Andrew's office, therefore, I took my slight luggage on board the steamboat for Portland, leaving letters and instructions with my sister Sarah, who was then my housekeeper at Concord, for her action in case I should find it expedient not to return home after a few days. The whole matter was so uncertain, and the action to be taken by the national authorities, and by the mass of the people, was so much in the dark, that it was impossible to say what might be the best course. I reached

F. B. SANBORN, 1860, ÆT 28
From a crayon by Miss H. Cheney)

EDWIN MORTON, 1885

HARRIET TUBMAN,
(A Fugitive Slave)

COL. JAMES MONTGOMERY

Quebec from Portland toward evening of Friday, the 21st, and that very afternoon Wendell Phillips wrote me the following note from Boston, which I did not receive for several days:

" MY DEAR FRIEND:

" I write more especially to inclose a copy of the conclusion to which John A. Andrew came, after looking up the law for our friend George Stearns. You see he thinks that parties who have *in Massachusetts* given aid to a treasonable act consummated in Virginia, would, if indicted, be tried in Massachusetts. This is different from the opinion he gave us in the afternoon [Thursday] and on which you based your action. I send you his exact words, and the whole of his paper, that you may have the whole before you—to see whether you will now change your plan and return. I have marked, at the close, the paragraph specially interesting to you.

John A. Andrew's Opinion (Oct. 21, 1859)

" ' In order to constitute the offence of " levying war," there must be more than a mere *conspiracy* to do it: some *overt act* of *war* must be committed.

" ' In order to constitute guilt (in any given person) of the overt act, he must be present at its commission. But he may be *constructively* present, though *actually* absent; that is to say, he may be remote from the principal scene of action, but performing some auxiliary or ancillary act,—such as keeping watch for the immediate actors, guarding them against surprise, having at hand for them means of escape, or the like; thus performing a part in that which constituted the overt act, or was immediately ancillary thereto.

" ' But a man cannot be held guilty of an overt act of

levying war, who was not present at the overt act of war; who participated in none of the transactions of the principal actors at the scene and did not, in any manner, render assistance, or attempt to do it, or put himself in a position where he might do so, if occasion offered at the time, nor perform any part in pursuance and in aid of the ends of the principal actors, anywhere, at the time of the overt act being committed.

" 'Still, if one joins in a conspiracy to levy war, and war is, afterwards, in fact levied, and he perform any act, which in the case of a felony, would render one an accessory, he thereby renders himself a principal to the treason, since, in treason all who are guilty at all are principals. Thus—if he gives arms, ammunition, horses or what not, to aid the war, pursuant to the conspiracy, such acts, when the war has been actually levied, will doubtless be deemed *overt acts* of treason, in themselves; but the party committing them can only be tried in the District where they were committed. A man who gave a cannon in Maine to the service of the cause of treason could not be tried for it in Texas, merely because it was in Texas, that other men, afterwards, fired it. But I think it would be regarded as of itself an act of treason, the war having been actually levied by other principal conspirators, for which he might be tried in Maine.'

" I asked J. A. A., 'Shall I write him that you think he had better return?' He replied, 'Send him what I have written, and let him decide for himself.'

" You know better than we what the precise contents of your letters were, and so can better judge; but, as you could not be carried hence as a witness, nor, if Andrew be correct, as an alleged criminal, you may think things are so changed that you'll return.

" George Stearns went to-day to see Emerson at Concord. They have kept the school going, and it will go ahead for a fortnight or more, awaiting your return. Emerson seemed, from what Stearns told me, to think you had done *wisely* in leaving.

" *No news* to-day. The young one we talked about * probably was there. Our *friend* who received telegrams has received one actor from the scene. The young Brown, whom we all saw last summer, is not dead. He was not there; letters have been received since from him; nothing in them important. Old man will probably recover, and I live in hope we'll see him again yet. Be sure we'll leave no stone unturned.

" If you write home while you deem it best to stay away, send your letters under cover to me, and tell them to send to me any letters for you, that I may mail them hence. It would not do to mail to you, even under an assumed name, or receive from you through a village post office."

(No signature.)

On Saturday, October 22, Phillips wrote me again, thus:

* This " young one " was Francis Jackson's grandson, Frank Merriam, who escaped from the Kennedy Farm with Owen Brown, and soon after came from Canada to his physician in Boston, Dr. David Thayer, living near Mr. Phillips. I cannot recall who was " our friend who received telegrams," unless it was Lewis Hayden, a Kentucky fugitive slave who long lived and died in Boston, where he finally served in the Legislature. The "actor from the scene" may have been a rather mythical John Anderson, whom Hayden enlisted for Brown, but who never got to the Ferry. John Brown, Jr., then living at Dorset, in Ohio, was the young Brown; the "old man " was Brown himself, badly wounded in the fray.

" DEAR FRIEND:

" I've not been able to get speech again with your *counsellor*, but *Worcester* [Higginson] and Dr. Howe and Emerson think there can be no risk to any one in your being here, and urge your *immediate* return. I concur in their opinion, and write at their request. Emerson says that at Concord they suppose you have gone south to Harper's Ferry. Perhaps it is as well to let them fancy so, and thus avoid the possibility of your absence directing attention to the real key of the movement.

" We are in motion with fresh plans, and need your counsel and knowledge of men and means. I wrote you yesterday by mail, and to-day telegraphed. No news."

Mr. Phillips was right in his theory that my little-noticed absence did not expose " the real key of the movement." That was in my hands, because most of the correspondence with Brown had passed by my hands and those of my classmate Morton, then in Gerrit Smith's family at Peterboro, N. Y. I had foreseen this in my flight to Canada, because I knew that without my answers the correspondence, if in the hands of Virginia, could not well be understood.* For this reason I early determined not to testify anywhere, silence being the best protection my implicated friends could have. I acted

* A well-informed, anonymous person in Boston, about the time I returned from Canada (Oct. 26), who evidently wished my testimony taken, wrote in a disguised hand this note to Governor Wise, who turned it over to Andrew Hunter, the prosecuting attorney at Charlestown, Va.:

" There are two persons in Masstts, and I think only two, who, if summoned as witnesses, can explain the whole of Brown's plot. Their names are Francis B. Sanborn of Concord & Rev. T. W. Higginson of Worcester, Mass. No time should be lost, as they may

on this theory afterward, and it was a suspicion
of the truth which made the Senate Committee in
the winter so eager to get me before Mason and
Jefferson Davis. I had left a certain discretion
with my sister, while giving her directions, and she
exercised discretion and courage as nobly in October as she did the next April, when she resisted
my kidnappers. I had written her at once from
Quebec, under my convenient name of Frederick
B. Stanley, and to this she replied on Sunday, October 23, the day following the second letter of
Phillips:

" My DEAR F.

"I got your letter last night. As I had previously,
on Friday, had a call from Mr. Emerson and Mr. Stearns,

abscond, but I do not think they will, as they think you would not
think it best to send for them.

A FRIEND OF ORDER.

[Endorsed]

 A Friend of Gov. Wise.

  Octo 1859.

  Call attention to this.

 Sent to me, now sent to you for what it
is worth.

H. A. W.

RICHMD Octo 29"

My college acquaintance, Major James Savage of Boston, whose
regiment occupied Charlestown for a while in the Civil War, found
this and other papers in Hunter's office in 1861-2, and sent them
home to his sister, Mrs. W. B. Rogers, who showed them to me at
the time. I thought I recognized the hand of this informer, and
asked permission to photograph the paper; but on reflection thought
better of it. I was then out of danger, and this "friend of order"
might have come to a new view of what "order" was; and I would
not undertake to expose him. It was singular that Higginson,
though active as Brown's friend, and quite a public character in
'59, which I was not, was not summoned before Hunter's court or
Mason's Committee. Like most Virginians of the period, Wise was

who thought the school should by all means go on for the present, I immediately went to see Mr. E. and had a consultation. By his advice, and almost *command*, I have suppressed the notes to Judge Hoar and Miss Waterman. He having seen Mr. Phillips and knowing Mr. Andrew's opinion, is strongly persuaded that you can return with safety, and will be here again in a few days. In the meantime the school is to go on with as little interruption as possible. I am to take all the classes I can, and help rule, if need be; Miss Waterman to take all the Latin but Lucretius; Ellen Emerson all the Greek except her own, and the German. It is thought that in this way all the scholars can be kept fully at work; and if this don't do, Mr. Emerson will immediately undertake to get a man—Mr. Abbot or some one, for a short time.

" Accepting his advice, and the opinion of your legal friends, I shall act as if your absence were to be only for a few days; and not at once attend to the various orders you have sent. Your absence thus far has not apparently

---

full of suspicions and very impulsive and changeable. On November 6 he wrote to Hunter:

" Better try Cook in your Court & turn Stevens over to Dist Ct of the U. S. But he may die & defeat ends of so turning him over. Cook is the worst of all these villians. I wish you to understand confidentially, that I will not reprieve or pardon one man *now* after the letters I have recd from the North. And as it may seem too severe for fair trial to put Stevens at bar let him be turned over."

But by December 18, seeing what a favorite Brown had become at the North and in Europe, he wrote to Hunter again:

" In reply to yours of the 15th I say definitively that Stevens ought *not* to be handed over, to the Federal authorities for trial. He is the deepest felon in guilt of all. I hope you informed the President exactly of the status of his case before the court. I am convinced that there is a political design in trying now to have him tried before the federal courts. He will not be delivered up with my consent."

created any particular sensation. Mr. Emerson's children think you have gone to aid in some way the prisoner. Miss Whiting told me in confidence that she thought you had gone to see Gerrit Smith. Mr. Emerson has promised to see Judge Hoar and confer with him. I have had some letters, all of which, except one from Miss Stephenson, I have done with as I thought best, after reading them. The one from Miss S. is marked *confidential*—therefore I neither read it nor send it without your order. I have taken care of E. Morton's letters, what there was about.

" I have ordered the coal, kept up the household arrangements as usual, and presented the same face to people as if all was going on peaceably. I am a little confused—stunned—at this great and sudden change; but am quite well, and do not bestow a thought on what people will say, even if the worst should come. Helen [our sister] is here, and will stay a few days longer. Julia [the faithful Irish servant] seems to realize that some mystery or misfortune is about us, though I don't know why. I have not written home, not wishing to disturb them too soon, nor to deal in uncertainties. I shall in a few days send to Charles [our brother, Dr. C. H. Sanborn] if he does not come here. I have not seen the Ripleys—and as no one knows that I am in pain, I do not have to submit to consolation. I don't like to have people think that your own safety was the principal motive for your going away; but if they do, there is no help for it.

" I have no doubt much good will come out of this to all immediately concerned, and don't consider that you need any vindication. I hope you will get through this all without breaking down. We have now and then apprehensions of somebody's coming to disturb things here, but do not believe there is much danger of that. I shall hope to hear from you very soon. Tell me whose writing is this slip—a friend who knew you first through Anna [Walker]. He writes without name about some letters of his.

"Good-bye. Yours truly,

"S. E. S."

I think this a model epistle. Of course I hastened back to Concord at once, and took up the daily routine of life as if nothing had happened. In the week of my absence I had formed the acquaintance of a young Catholic priest at the Jesuit College in Quebec, had spent hours reading in the library, of which he was the custodian, and had made the reading acquaintance of Lucan's "Pharsalia" and the quaint biographies of Izaak Walton and Mrs. Colonel Hutchinson. My coming was hastened by this laconic note from Emerson:

"By all means return at the first hour wheels or steam will permit. I assure every one that you shall be here Wednesday or Thursday.

"Sunday Night.   Yours ever, R. W. E."

I had not been many days returned, when Colonel Charles Miller, a classmate of the poet Lowell at Harvard, and the son-in-law of Gerrit Smith, appeared at my door one afternoon, to bring me word that Morton had sailed for England from Quebec; that Mr. Smith was in the Utica Insane Asylum, or soon would be, and that my letters to Morton were buried under a brick in the broad walk leading to Mr. Smith's hall-door. In return he would learn what I had done with Mr. Smith's letters? I told him they were destroyed, so far as I could find them. He had been on a similar errand to John Brown, Jr., in Ohio, and was much relieved at what I told him. In fact, however, several of Smith's letters concerning John Brown had lodged either with Wentworth Higginson or Theodore Parker, to whom I had sent them, and they did afterward come back into my possession or use. A requisition for Mr. Smith from the governor of Virginia, as an accomplice of Brown, was received by the governor of New York, quite early in the excitement, and Morton had visited Albany to learn what was to be done about it. He did not see Governor Morgan, but a person quite as effective for the government of New York— Thurlow Weed, who expressed to Morton the wish that Gerrit Smith were in Canada. Morton took the hint and went to Quebec, whence he sailed for England; but Mr. Smith found a safer asylum at Utica, with Dr. Gray. Dr. Howe and Mr. Stearns took a temporary refuge in Canada, as I had done, and was to do again, when the Senate of the United States, in the next winter, voted my arrest. But I now remained at home, or in Boston and Concord, made my usual round of visits; took part in the duty of raising money for the family of Brown, and met Mrs. Brown in Boston, when Higginson escorted her down from the Adirondac forest in November, to make her way from New England to Virginia, to take the last farewell of her husband in Charlestown. As she was on her journey from Burlington, Vt., November 4, I got this note from Higginson, to which I gave instant attention:

"BURLINGTON, Thursday A. M.

"DEAR FRIEND:

"Mrs. Brown will reach the American House, Boston, at 8 P. M. I have telegraphed Howe to call on her there to-night, and to ask Stearns to go to Philadelphia with her—as I have been away four days, and she is not good at traveling. She is a noble woman, and the whole family are in the finest state of mind. I have telegraphed Russell and Sennott * for leave to her to visit her husband. She goes via Boston for several reasons. I shall go to Worcester to-night, and Boston to-morrow A. M. to see about her. She should go on to-morrow with somebody. Can't you come to Boston to-morrow?

"T. W. H."

I went as requested, and there renewed my acquaintance with John Brown's wife. I also telegraphed to Miller McKim, in Philadelphia, to meet her there, to which he thus made answer:

"PHILA., Nov. 5,

"DEAR SIR:

"Your telegram of yesterday came in due time. I have been at the Wharf this morning, but thus far (it is now 12.30 P. M.) she has not made her appearance, or, if she has, I have not recognized her. She will probably arrive here in the next boat, which gets here at two o'clock— but I have an appointment to speak at an anti-slavery meeting, which will prevent me from meeting her. My friend Passmore Williamson, however, will be on hand and

---

* Thomas Russell and George Sennott, from Boston—both then in Charlestown to befriend Brown.

CABIN OF OWEN AND JASON BROWN, NEAR PASADENA, 1880
Owen in the doorway

FUNERAL OF OLIVER BROWN AND OTHERS AT NORTH ELBA, 1900

pay her the attention which she may require. James Red-path will also delay his departure for New York till the 6 o'clock train this evening, in order to meet her. He desires me to say this to you.

"Regretting not to be able to meet Mrs. Brown, and hoping to be of service in some other way, if you should have need of my offices, I am, dear sir,

"Yours truly,

"J. M. McKim."

Mrs. Brown found good friends all along her way, going and coming, except in Maryland and Virginia; but even there she was treated with courtesy. Governor Wise, who did not wish any of the invaders of Virginia to be buried in that sacred soil, and who had sent the body of her son Watson to a medical college for preservation as a specimen of anatomy, allowed her to take her husband for burial at North Elba. Meanwhile the friends of Brown were raising money for the aid of the family, and were expressing some anxiety about the arrest of those who had aided the foray. Emerson, writing from his favorite hotel in Boston, the American House, November 9, had this to say to me:

"My dear Sir:

"Would it not be better that you should take legal counsel at this time, by explicitly stating your liabilities, if any exist, to a counsellor? I was talking this morning with Mr. [John M.] Forbes, who looked with some uneasiness at the telegraphic despatch of this morning, and afterward I had a little conversation with Judge Hoar.

The Judge does not overestimate the United States power, yet could answer no question in the dark. And it is only on the contingency that there may be anything in your case not known or probable to them, that the suggestion can have any importance.

" I have been talking with a few persons on the possibility of finding any gentleman here who might have private influence with Gov. Wise for Capt. Brown, and am to see others in the morning.

"Yours ever,

"R. W. EMERSON."

I was not inclined to unbosom myself to any lawyer, in advance of some necessity for it, which I did not then see; and Rockwood Hoar, being a sitting judge in our State court, could not properly hear my case in advance. As to the suggestion of an envoy to Virginia, I replied (Nov. 10, 1859) :

" There is hope in every effort to save Brown—but not much, as it would seem, in the representations of a private gentleman to Governor Wise, who is in this matter the servant of others. It is the *Bellua multorum capitum* of Virginia that will execute the sentence if it is done; and *that* is perhaps implacable. *Escape*, difficult as it seems, is probably Brown's best chance for life. If a reprieve, or an arrest of judgment for another month were possible, a rescue would not be so hard to manage. Brown's heroic character is having its influence on his keepers, as we learn; but at present he does not *wish* to escape."

Such was indeed the fact; Brown refused to be rescued by force, since it might involve his jailer, John Avis, in death or reproach. But when I got back to Concord from Canada, October 26, I had found much in agitation there, as will be seen by these passages in Alcott's Diary:

" *Oct. 26, Evening.* See Sanborn at Emerson's house; he has come home from looking into Capt. Brown's affairs. He was Brown's friend and entertained him here last May, as well as on a former visit in 1857. Ellery Channing is at Emerson's also, and we discuss the matter at length, I defending the deed, under the circumstances, and the *Man.* His rescue would be difficult, even if he would consent to be taken. And the spectacle of a martyrdom such as his must needs be, will be of greater service to the country, and to the coming in of a righteous rule, than years of agitation by the Press, or the voices of partisans, North and South. 'Twas a bold stroke, this of his, for justice universal, and it damages all (political) parties beyond repair. Even the Republicans must in some sense claim him as theirs in self-defense, and to justify Republicanism in the people's eyes as Freedom's defender.

" *Wednesday, 9th November.* Thoreau calls on me at the Orchard House. He thinks some one from the North should see Gov. Wise, or write concerning Brown's character and motives, to influence the governor in his favor. Thoreau is the man to write, or Emerson. But there seems little or no hope of pleas for mercy. Slavery must have its way and Wise must do its bidding on peril of his own safety.

" *Nov. 28, Evening.* At the Town Hall, a meeting being called there to make arrangements for celebrating by appropriate services the day of Captain Brown's execution. Simon Brown, Dr. Bartlett, Keyes, Emerson and Thoreau addressed the meeting; and Emerson, Thoreau, Brown and Keyes are chosen a committee to prepare the

service proper for the occasion. Sanborn is present also.
Thoreau has taken a prominent part in the movement
and chiefly arranged for it.

"*Nov. 30.* See Thoreau again, and Emerson, concerning the Brown services on Friday, Dec. 2. We do not
intend to have any speeches made on the occasion, but
have selected appropriate passages from Brown's words,
from the Poets and from the Scriptures, to be read by
Thoreau, Emerson and myself, chiefly. The selection and
arrangement is ours. *Dec. 1.* Again see Thoreau and
Emerson. It is understood that I am to read the Martyr's Service, Thoreau the selections from the poets and
Emerson those from Brown's words. I copy the passages
I am to read from the Wisdom of Solomon, David's
Psalms and also from Plato. Sanborn has written a
dirge, which will be sung, and Rev. E. H. Sears from
Wayland, will offer prayer."

On the day of Brown's execution, December 2,
a beautiful mild winter day, suitable for boating
on our Concord River, these arrangements made
by Alcott (who was then our town superintendent
of schools), by Emerson, Thoreau, J. S. Keyes,
afterward U. S. Marshal, and Simon Brown, who
had been lieutenant-governor, were appropriately
carried out in the presence of a large audience.
The whole service was afterward published by
Redpath in his "Echoes of Harper's Ferry," and
the manuscript is in my possession, written in the
various hands of the authors, and of Miss Ellen
Emerson, who copied some portions.* My Dirge

---

* Mr. Alcott's Diary (Dec. 2, 1859) says: " Ellen Emerson sends
me her fair copy of the Martyr Service. At 2 P. M. we meet at

Service for the Death of
a Martyr. Read by A. B.
Alcott.

(Christ.)

"

Whatsoever ye would that

men should do to you, do ye

even so to them; for this is

the law and the prophets. "

"

whether it be lawful to

obey God or man judge

ye. " —

AUTOGRAPHS OF THOREAU AND ALCOTT

was sung by the whole congregation, and an ode
of mine was also read; but so careful were my
townsmen that I should not be prejudiced by the
publication of my name, that I was described
merely as a "gentleman of Concord." I was present, and so was Rev. E. H. Sears of Wayland,
Mrs. Emerson's favorite clergyman then, who, on
the smooth cover of his prayer-book, wrote these
prophetic lines, as the service proceeded:

> " Not any spot six feet by two
>   Will hold a man like thee;
> John Brown will tramp the shaking earth
>   From Blue Ridge to the sea,
> Till the strong angel come at last
>   And opes each dungeon door,
> And God's Great Charter holds and waves
>   O'er all his humble poor."

George Hoyt, of Athol, who had bravely gone
to Charlestown to assist in the defense of Brown,
had by this time returned home, and wrote me, December 9, a warning letter, after a conversation
with him, in which I rather slighted his fears for
me. He said:

" I feel it my duty to point out the dangers, even if I
cannot prevail on you to avoid them. It is probable you
already see the new trap which Senator Mason has set
for you. His resolution of inquiry empowers the com-

the Town Hall, our own townspeople present mostly, and many
from the adjoining towns. Simon Brown is chairman; the readings
are by Thoreau, Emerson, C. Bowers, and Alcott; and Sanborn's
' Dirge ' is sung by the company,

mittee of the Senate to send for persons and papers. Once in the city of Washington, a witness before that committee, it will be easy to take you into Virginia. If you avoid anything, you must shun the process of this committee of investigation. Mason is an old fox."

A postscript fixes the date before which F. J. Merriam, who escaped with Owen Brown from the Kennedy Farm, must have been in Boston and at my house in Concord; where I declined to see him (out of regard for his safety), though I gave him shelter and sent him on to safety in Canada. Hoyt writes:

"Merriam, whom I saw when he last visited Boston, was chagrined at your lack of confidence in his judgment. I think him clearly insane."

During November there had been serious anxieties felt by some of our friends, of the kind mentioned by Hoyt; and Dr. Howe, in a letter of November 14, had pointed out to the public a possible danger arising under laws of which most persons were ignorant. The precise danger is specified in a letter of mine to Higginson, of November 13, thus:

"I had a talk with Andrew last night, who showed me the statute about witnesses. It appears by a law of August 8, 1846, a witness whose evidence is deemed *material* by any U. S. judge, may be arrested by a warrant from a judge, without any previous summons, and taken before that judge to give bond for his appearing to testify. This leaves no room for a writ of *habeas corpus*, unless the State judges are willing to take the ground that the statute is unconstitutional, or that it means the process shall run only within the judge's district or circuit; and Andrew does not believe (nor do I) that our judges are ready to take either ground. Therefore, if arrested, a witness can only be released by a tumult. This may do very well in Worcester, but is rather precarious in Boston; and therefore Phillips thinks there should be some concert of action between those likely to be arrested. Would your Worcester people go down to Boston to take Dr. Howe or Wendell Phillips out of the marshal's hands?"

On the 19th I added a statement of my own position, in a letter to Higginson dealing with some other matters:

" I shall pursue my usual occupations, or any that I may take up, whatever summons or other process may be issued; shall resist arrest by force, shall refuse to sue a writ of *habeas corpus*,—but, if arrested, shall consent to be rescued only by force. It is possible the anxiety of friends may induce me to modify this course, but I think not. I have to-night had a long talk with Judge Hoar, from which I infer that this particular statute of 1846 would be resisted by his court; but that no resistance would be made to an ordinary summons and capias. There is no hope in the courts at present; but the *people* can prevent the execution of this law. This is why I shall refuse any writ of *habeas corpus*.

" Talking of a rescue for Brown, have you gone any farther in that matter? and can anything be done? Alcott is ready to go on and get communication with Capt.

Brown, if that is thought best; and he could perhaps do so—he better than most persons. Write me what you think of this. I shall probably be in Boston on Friday and Saturday after Thanksgiving, if not before; perhaps I may come to Worcester in my vacation—or I may go southward or westward."

Nothing came of this alarm about the old law; but, as Hoyt had written me, it was feared that Mason's summons might be used to get obnoxious persons into Virginia; and when John Brown, Jr., was summoned before Mason, as I was early in January, 1860, he declined to go to Washington; first, because he would be liable to seizure in passing through Virginia or Maryland; and next, because he would not testify against others at the price of his own exemption. I received no previous assurance from Mason, but when I offered to testify in Massachusetts, through fear of lack of protection in Washington, Mason assured me that he would be personally responsible for my safety. I was not so much concerned for that as resolved never to testify before slaveholders in regard to my friends.

Senator Mason refused my proposal to testify in Massachusetts, as I supposed he would, and I then wrote him that under no conditions would I appear before his committee, but throw myself on my rights as a citizen of Massachusetts; reminding him also that I could hardly rely on his offer of protection, since my friend, Senator Sumner, had been brutally assaulted a few years earlier, in the

Senate chamber itself. Upon the receipt of this missive, Mason reported me to the Senate as a contumacious witness, and my arrest was voted, February 16, 1860, as that of John Brown, Jr., and James Redpath was. A few of the Southern Senators, seeing that my attitude about State Rights was quite similar to theirs, voted against my arrest, and began to send me their political speeches. Not choosing to be seized before I was quite ready, I retired again to Canada, in the latter part of February, taking North Elba in my northward route, in order to see the Brown family, and to make arrangements for two of Brown's daughters, Anne and Sarah, to enter my school, as they did, in March.

CHAPTER VIII

Personal Replevin

WHEN I had written and forwarded to the Vice-President and to my friend, Senator Hale, of New Hampshire, my protest against the Senate's unlawful action, as I viewed it, I returned to Concord, and went about my business as usual, besides frequent visits to Boston and lecturing in New Hampshire. After so long an interval, with no effort at arresting me, I concluded that the Senate officials had given up their purpose of taking me to Washington, as they would have done had they been wise. But on the evening of April 3, 1860, after I had been out making calls in the village of Concord, and was sitting quietly in my study on the first floor, after nine o'clock, my door-bell rang.

Our one servant, Julia Leary, had gone to bed. My sister Sarah, who was still my housekeeper, was in her chamber, and, without anticipating any harm, I went down into the front hall and answered the bell. A young man presented himself and handed me a note, which I stepped back to read by the light of the hall lamp. It said that the bearer was a person deserving charity, and I am satisfied that he was so before he got away from Concord that night. When I looked up from reading the note, four men had entered my hall, and one of them, Silas Carleton by name (a Boston tipstaff, as I afterward learned), came forward and laid his hand on me, saying, " I arrest you."

I said, " By what authority? If you have a warrant read it, for I shall not go with you unless you show your warrant."

Carleton, or the youth who had begged my charity, then began to read the order of the Senate for my arrest. But my sister, who had feared, as I did not, what this visit meant, now rushed down the stairs, opened the other door of the hall and began to alarm the neighbors. Seeing that they were likely to be interrupted in their mission, my five callers then folded up their warrant, slipped a pair of handcuffs on my wrists before I suspected what they were doing, and tried to force me from the house.

I was young and strong and resented this indignity. They had to raise me from the floor and began to carry me (four of them) to the door where my sister stood, raising a constant alarm. My hands were powerless, but as they approached the door I braced my feet against the posts and delayed them. I did the same at the posts of the veranda, and it was some minutes before they got me on the gravel walk at the foot of my stone steps. Meanwhile, the church bells were ringing a fire alarm, and the people were gathering by tens. At the stone posts of the gateway I checked their progress once more, and again, when the four rascals lifted me to insert me, feet foremost, in their carriage (a covered hack with a driver on the box), I braced myself against the sides of the carriage door and broke them in. By this time it was re-vealed to them that my unfettered feet were mak-ing all this trouble, and one of the four, named Tarleton, wearing a long black beard, grasped my feet and brought them together, so that I could no longer use them in resistance. They had got me into their hack as far as my knees, when my sister, darting forward, grasped the long beard of my footman and pulled with so much force that the pain of it compelled him to lose his grasp, and my feet felt the ground again, outside of the carriage.

Now while all this was going on a great crowd had collected, among them old Colonel Whiting, with his daughter Anne, and his stout cane, with which he began to beat the horses; while Miss Whit-ing climbed to the box beside the driver, and as-sured him that she was going as far as he and his horses went. They began to start at the repeated strokes of the good colonel's cane, and my bearers were left a rod or two behind the hack into which they had not been able to force me. They saw at once that their kidnapping game was defeated, but they still held me, hatless and in my evening slip-pers, in the street in front of my house.

At that moment, my counsel, J. S. Keyes, ap-peared by my side, asking me if I petitioned for a writ of habeas corpus. "By all means," said I, and he hurried off to the house of Judge Hoar, some twenty rods away.

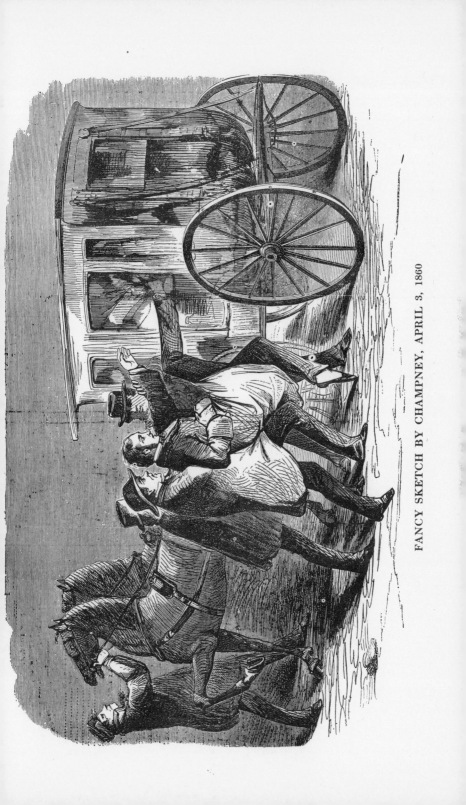

FANCY SKETCH BY CHAMPNEY, APRIL 3, 1860

The judge, hearing the tumult, and suspecting what it was, went to his library and began filling out the proper blank for the great writ of personal replevin. In less than ten minutes after my verbal petition the writ was in the hands of the stalwart deputy sheriff, John Moore, who at once made the formal demand on my captors to surrender their prisoner. Stupidly, as they had acted all along, they refused.

The sheriff then called on the 150 men and women present to act as his *posse comitatus,* which some twenty of the men gladly did, and I was forcibly snatched from senatorial custody. At the same time my Irish neighbors rushed upon them and forced them to take to their broken carriage, and make off toward Lexington, the way they had driven up in the early evening. They were pursued by twenty or thirty of my townsmen, some of them as far as Lexington, but got away with no very serious bruises.

I was committed to the custody of Captain George L. Prescott (in the Civil War, Colonel Prescott, killed at Petersburg) and spent the night in his house not far from the Old Manse, armed, for my better defense, with a six-shooter, which Mr. Bull, the inventor of the Concord grape (then chairman of the selectmen), insisted I should take. I slept peacefully all the rest of that night, from about 11 o'clock, when the fray ended.

In the morning I was taken to Boston by Sheriff Moore and carried to the old court house, near the present City Hall, where the justices of the Supreme Court were holding a law term. My counsel, who volunteered for the case, were John A. Andrew, soon afterward Governor; Samuel Sewall, a cousin of Mrs. Alcott, and my college classmate, Robert Treat Paine. The case was argued by Andrew and Sewall in my behalf, and by C. L. Woodbury, son of the distinguished Justice Levi Woodbury, of New Hampshire, who had been dead for some years, but whose son was the Democratic district attorney.

The court room was filled with my Concord and Boston friends, among them Wendell Phillips and Walt Whitman; and in the afternoon Chief Justice Shaw, the most eminent jurist in New England, delivered the following decision, setting me free:

OPINION OF THE SUPREME JUDICIAL COURT.

F. B. Sanborn vs. Silas Carleton.

SHAW, C. J. This arrest was made by Silas Carleton, a citizen and inhabitant of Massachusetts; and in his answer under oath, he shows a warrant to Dunning R. McNair, sergeant-at-arms of the Senate of the United States, and says that the sergeant-at-arms entered an order upon it, delegating the power to Carleton to make the arrest. There is therefore no conflict in this case between the authority of an executive officer of the United States and an officer of this Commonwealth.

It appears by the answer of the officer, which stands as part of the return to the writ of *habeas corpus*, that Carleton claims to have arrested Sanborn under a warrant purporting to have been issued under the hand and seal of the vice-president of the United States and president of the Senate. It recites the appointment of a committee of the Senate to inquire into the circumstances of the attack made by a body of men upon the arsenal of the United States at Harper's Ferry; the citation of Sanborn to answer as a witness before such committee; that he refused to attend according to such summons; that he was thereby guilty of a contempt; and directing Dunning R. McNair, sergeant-at-arms of the Senate, to arrest the said Sanborn, wherever he could find him, and bring him before the Senate to answer for such contempt. This warrant seems to have been issued on the 16th of February last. There is an indorsement of the same date, by the sergeant-at-arms, authorizing and empowering the said Carleton, the respondent, to make such arrest; and the respondent justifies the arrest made on the 3d April, instant, under that process. The question is whether this arrest is justified by this return.

This question is a very broad and a very important one, and opens many interesting questions as to the functions and powers of the United States Senate, as a constituent part both of the legislative and executive departments of the United States government; and the modes in which they are to be exercised, and the limits by which they are qualified.

It is admitted in the arguments that there is no express provision in the Constitution of the United States, giving this authority in terms; but it is maintained that it is necessarily incidental to various authorities vested in the Senate of the United States, in its legislative, executive and judicial functions, and must therefore be held to be conferred by necessary implication.

These questions manifestly requiring great deliberation and research in order to come to a satisfactory conclusion, and some preliminary questions having been suggested by the petitioner's counsel, it was proposed, and not objected to by the learned district attorney and assistant district attorney of the United States, by whom the court were attended in behalf of the respondent, to consider these preliminary questions first; because, if the objections, on the face of them, were sustained, it would supersede the necessity of discussing the other questions arising in the case. These points have been argued.

For obvious reasons, we lay out of this inquiry the case of the Senate, when acting in their judicial capacity, on the trial of an impeachment laid before them by the House of Representatives; and we suppose the same considerations would apply to the case of the House of Representatives in summoning witnesses to testify before them, as the grand inquest of the United States, with a view to an impeachment.

Then the objections taken to this warrant, as apparent on the face of it, as rendering it insufficient to justify the arrest of the petitioner, are three:

1. That the sergeant-at-arms, in his capacity as an officer of the Senate, had no authority to execute process out of the limits of the District of Columbia, over which the United States have, by the Constitution, exclusive jurisdiction.

2. That a sergeant-at-arms is not an officer known to the Constitution or laws of the United States, as a general executive, of known powers, like a sheriff or marshal; that he is appointed and recognized by the rules of the Senate as an officer exercising powers regulated by the rules and orders of the Senate, and can only exercise such powers as are conferred on him by such general rules and orders, made with a view to the regular proceedings of the Senate; or such as may be conferred by the Sen-

ate by special resolves and acts, as a single department of the government, without the concurrence of the other members of the government.

3. That by the warrant returned, the power to arrest the respondent was in terms limited to McNair, the sergeant-at-arms, and could not be executed by a deputy.

In regard to the first, it seems to us that the objection assumes a broader ground than it is necessary to occupy in deciding this preliminary question. We are not prepared to say that in no case can the Senate direct process to be served beyond the limits of the district, by an authority expressly given for that purpose.

The case of *Anderson* v. *Dunn*, 6 Wheat. 204, cited in the argument, has little application to this question. It is manifest that that was a writ of error from the circuit court for the District of Columbia, and it appears that the alleged contempt of Anderson, in offering a bribe to a member of the House of Representatives, was committed in the District of Columbia, the act complained of as the trespass was done therein, and the process in question was served therein. In that case the process was served by the sergeant-at-arms in person, under an express authority given by the House of Representatives, by their resolve for that purpose, in pursuance of which the speaker's warrant was issued.

The second question appears to us far more material. The sergeant-at-arms of the Senate is an officer of that house, like their doorkeeper, appointed by them, and required by their rules and orders to exercise certain powers, mainly with a view to order and due course of proceeding. He is not a general officer, known to the law, as a sheriff, having power to appoint general deputies, or to act by special deputation in particular cases; nor like a marshal, who holds analogous powers, and possesses similar functions, under the laws of the United States, to those of sheriffs and deputies under the State laws.

But even where it appears, by the terms or the reasonable construction of a statute, conferring an authority on a sheriff, that it was intended he should execute it personally, he cannot exercise it by general deputy, and of course he cannot do it by special deputation. *Wood* v. *Ross*, 11 Mass. 271.

But, upon the third point, the court are all of opinion that the warrant affords no justification. Suppose that the Senate had authority, by the resolves passed by them, to cause the petitioner to be arrested and brought before them, it appears by the warrant issued for that purpose that the power was given alone to McNair, sergeant-at-arms, and there is nothing to indicate any intention on their part to have such arrest made by any other person. There is no authority, in fact, given by this warrant to delegate the authority to any other person. It is a general rule of the common law, not founded on any judicial decision or statute provision, but so universally received as to have grown into a maxim, that a delegated authority to one does not authorize him to delegate it to another. *Delegata potestas non potest delegari.* Broom's Maxim's (3d ed.) 755. This grows out of the nature of the subject. A special authority is in the nature of a trust. It implies confidence in the ability, skill or discretion of the party intrusted. The author of such a power may extend it if he will, as is done in ordinary powers of attorney, giving power to one or his substitute or substitutes to do the acts authorized. But when it is not so extended it is limited to the person named.

The counsel for the respondent asked what authority there is for limiting such warrant to the person named; it rather belongs to those who wish to justify under such delegated power, to show judicial authority for the extension.

On the special ground that this respondent had no legal authority to make the arrest, and has now no legal authority to detain the petitioner in his custody, the order of the court is that the *said Sanborn be discharged from the custody of said Carleton.*

I was then taken by enthusiastic friends to East Cambridge in a carriage (to avoid rearrest in Boston), and from there returned to Concord, where a public meeting was held that evening to protest against the outrage offered to a citizen and to the town. No further effort was made to arrest me, the time and manner of my seizure having put the public opinion of Massachusetts wholly on my side. Citizens of Boston presented my sister with a handsome revolver in recognition of her tact and courage. The next September I had the satisfaction of helping to nominate Mr. Andrew for governor of Massachusetts in the Worcester Convention, to which I was sent as a Concord delegate. We elected and reëlected him, and three years later he appointed me secretary of the Board of State Charities, a new and important office.

This year, 1860, was the last of Judge Shaw's life, and he had no opportunity, even had he wished it, to modify this decision. It agreed with the sentiments of two-thirds of the people of Massachusetts, and made me popular in quarters where I was not known before. The Democratic marshal of New Hampshire, a distant cousin of mine, sent me word that, if I chose to visit my native State, he should not be able to find me, in case a second warrant for my arrest should issue. But I had no occasion to accept his suggestion, being from that time forward as safe from arrest as the marshals themselves. Indeed, I brought suit against the five kidnappers who visited Concord, and also had them indicted at the next term of the Middlesex County Court for the criminal offense of kidnapping, which had been carefully defined in our laws. But the Civil War coming on, early in 1861, and several of my kidnappers, with their counsel (General B. F. Butler), having volunteered or gone to the front, I withdrew my suit, and requested the district attorney to *nol pros.* the indictment.

CHAPTER IX

Aftermath of the John Brown Foray

SO important and so thrilling an interlude in my youthful life as the John Brown Foray, not merely into Missouri and Virginia, but into world-history, could not occur without leaving with me deep impressions; and it was followed by an aftermath of events and consequences. "To be in a plot," said Cardinal de Retz, speaking of his early conspiracy to assassinate Cardinal Richelieu, "is often a mark of folly; but nothing is more likely to make a man wise, at least for a time, than to have been in one. The reason is that the danger still subsists, after the opportunity is lost, which requires more prudence and circumspection than ordinary in one's behavior." I fancy that this result occurred in my own case, and that the confidence reposed in one so young as I was, in 1858, was partly in consequence of the habit of thought and feeling which this adventure strengthened in me. But I cannot say, with that cardinal, in the same connection, "Yet I wish with all my heart that I had never been in that plot"; for I have never in the least regretted my small share in Brown's enterprise. What was my feeling at the time, when the ill consequences to myself, present or prospective, were in full view during the winter of 1859-60, may be seen by the letters I wrote to my mother, who, approaching sixty, and with many reasons for anxiety on other accounts, was naturally in need of assurance and comfort. December 1, the day before the execution of Brown, and of the funeral service in his honor at Concord, I wrote to her from Concord thus:

" My dear Mother:

" I was meaning to come home to Hampton Falls at Thanksgiving, but Helen wrote it was not advisable,— and after that I made engagements hereabouts which kept me. Now I may come, but not till Monday, if at all. My school begins on Wednesday, December 7th, and I have the town schools and my domestic matters to look after in this vacation. But I shall come if I can, and if not now, then some Sunday in the winter.

" From the newspapers and the other accounts of me and my connection with Captain Brown, very likely you may feel some anxiety about me; and I will explain why there is no occasion for alarm. In the first place, there is no evidence against me as a criminal, in any fair court; the only way of arresting me will be as a witness. Now the law of 1846, which allows witnesses to be suddenly arrested and carried out of the State, cannot be enforced here, because the Supreme Court will prevent it; and no officer would venture to kidnap a man. The ordinary process for summoning a witness is slow, and would give me time to escape, if I wished to do so. I don't intend, however, to be arrested, and I think I can avoid it without escaping. At any rate, the trials for which they want my evidence do not come on until May; and they will not, naturally, summon the witnesses until April, before which time there may be many changes. Even if I went as a witness, I would be under the United States protection,—and without violating the law they could not harm me.

"But I do not think it at all probable they will even attempt to arrest me, and I feel no fear of it. Dr. Howe has left the country, it is true; but I think he will soon return. I went to Canada when I did, not so much to avoid arrest, as to prevent the obtaining of information; and, unless I meant to flee the country altogether, should not go there again.

"What I have really done to aid Brown is nothing more than all men ought to do; and it will bring only glory to me hereafter, if not now. I am sorry to give my friends, and especially you, so much anxiety; but otherwise I have never for a moment regretted my connection with the affair. If my name is remembered at all in it, it will be in an honorable way. The fruits of Brown's acts are to be a great good, I have no doubt. I shall take no active part in our meeting here to-morrow, nor do anything imprudent if I can avoid it.

"So you must keep up good courage, and remember that the worst part of it all, to me, is to have others suffer on my account. My school goes on well, and I am likely to have more scholars than ever this winter. If I come on Monday (December 5), I shall send you word that morning; but I doubt if I can come conveniently.

"Yours affectionately,
"FRANK B. SANBORN."

At the writing of this the Senate Committee's action was not foreseen. That changed the method of procedure, but did not otherwise affect my mind.

I was summoned in January, as already mentioned, and by the Marshal himself in the Concord post-office, a Democratic headquarters. I refused to obey the summons, and the Senate voted my arrest. But I could not believe that prudent men, such as I thought the slave oligarchy to be, would add to the excitement of the North by arresting me. I retired to Canada to prepare my protest and to visit the Brown family on the way, as I did; and on my return to Concord I wrote my mother again, February 28, 1860, as follows:

" You see by the date of my letter that I am still here, though in a place unknown to all but a few persons. [It was the house of Colonel Whiting, near my school.] I *think* I might have been about just as freely as usual, since my arrest was ordered by the Senate; but to be on the safe side I have taken these precautions. It is not generally known even that I am in town, though I was walking in the street every evening but one last week, and on Sunday walked all around town, and called at half a dozen houses. I keep myself busy indoors with reading and writing, and keep an eye on my school, which goes on very well in my absence, under Mr. Whittemore and the other teachers. I am very well, though I wish I had a little more exercise.

" You have seen, I suppose, my petition to the Senate, which was yesterday presented by Senator Hale, of New Hampshire. The objections made in it to the Senate's authority are no doubt good, and will seem so to people, the more they are examined and discussed. I do not think the Senate will assent to them; but neither do I think they will carry the matter so far as to arrest me. They and the country are tired of the whole thing, and will get

it off their hands as soon as convenient I believe.   I
shall not leave the country, nor even this State, as I now
think; and I conclude I shall be left at liberty to go about
my business in a few weeks.   I doubt very much if any
warrant for my arrest has been issued by the Vice-President,—for I can hear of none such.   Even if I should be
arrested it would be only a nominal detention, I think.

"So I hope you will not be concerned about me; for
I am as unconcerned as ever in my life; and while I do
not mean to give up a single point to the Senate, I expect to be unmolested for the future.   Sarah is as well
as usual, and Julia still keeps house for me.   I slept
at home last Saturday night.   The Brown girls, Anne
and Sarah, daughters of John Brown, wt. t to school
yesterday."

This confidence on my part was not assumed,
for I actually could not suppose the partisans of
the Buchanan administration unwise enough to arrest me, and give me the advantage of the public
sympathy, which that would surely excite.   But
the folly of the pro-slavery party was beyond cal-
culation; and their agents not only served their
long-withheld warrant early in April, but did it
in the dark, and with circumstances of outrage.
When I had been discharged from arrest by Chief
Justice Shaw, April 4, 1860, I wrote again to my
mother, dating from Concord, April 6:

"You have seen by the papers the state of affairs in
my case, and how entirely we have defeated the out-
rageous purpose of the ruffians who came to seize me.
I have slept every night in Concord, and every night
but one in my own house; and shall remain here and

pursue my duties,—feeling very little apprehension for
the future. The people defended me, and will again.
Charles (Dr. Sanborn) is here to-day, also George Walker
and other friends of mine; and the four ruffians are held
to bail for kidnapping. I shall also sue them for damages,
and hope to build my schoolhouse out of their money.
" I am well, and was not much hurt in the affray.
Sarah also is pretty well, though tired. She has become
quite a lioness by the means."

With the rest of the intimate friends of Brown,
affairs took various courses. Dr. Howe and Mr.
Stearns testified before Mason's committee, during
the winter, and so did other witnesses. Edwin
Morton went to Europe, as a means of protecting
Gerrit Smith, and there renewed his acquaintance
with Thomas Cholmondeley, Thoreau's friend, at
Shrewsbury and Hodnet, besides making new acquaintances in England and France; but he returned in the summer of 1860, and commenced the
study of law in Plymouth. Gerrit Smith by this
time was discharged from the Utica insane asylum,
and maintained his attitude of admiration for
Brown and ignorance of his plans. The Civil
War came on, and gave the country much else
to think of. My school dwindled in consequence
of the war, and in 1863 I accepted the invitation
of Mr. Stearns to succeed Moncure Conway in
the editorship of the *Commonwealth,* an emancipation weekly in Boston. I was often in consultation with Morton (who had recovered from a
long illness, and begun the practice of law in Bos-

Boston. Ap. 13   186 .

My Dear Sir,

do you
want any watchers
on attendants?
If I can be of any
service, in any way
I shall be ready
with what little of
strength & energy
is left.

Faithfully

S G Howe.

ton), as to how we should best preserve the true story of Brown's Virginia plans, which the unwillingness of Mr. Smith to avow his connection with the scheme, had left in much uncertainty as to the actual facts. Finally, in 1871, after the happy conclusion of the Civil War, Morton and I agreed that I should write for the *Atlantic Monthly* an anonymous article, stating the general facts as we both knew them. This was done, and led to a painful correspondence with the Smiths, the general result of which was published by me in the New York *Critic* some years ago. What is essential will here be reproduced. It may be stated that Mr. Stearns had died in 1867; Mr. Smith died in 1874, Dr. Howe in 1876, and Morton, at his Swiss retirement in Morges, on the lake of Geneva, in 1900.

The late Octavius Frothingham's first edition of Gerrit Smith's biography in 1878 led to a sharp controversy in the New York journals concerning the statements made therein about Mr. Smith's connection with the plans of John Brown for attacking negro slavery by force. At that time, anticipating that I might be called to declare in public the facts within my knowledge, but very unwilling to appear in the controversy, I wrote a letter to the New York *Evening Post,* which was to be my statement for those who wished to learn the truth. Circumstances so turned out—charges against me personally having been withdrawn by General John Cochrane, a nephew of Mr. Smith, upon my showing him the autograph letters—that

I had no need to make disclosures in 1878. Since then, the death of most of the persons cognizant of the facts, and likely to be pained by such a disclosure, make it possible for me to publish what I long held back, at the request, as will be seen, of friends whose wishes I could not disregard, unless it became absolutely necessary, in the interest of historical truth. I here subjoin so much of my letter to the *Post* as the lapse of time and change of circumstances have not rendered needless:

THE LETTER OF MARCH 15, 1878

To the Editor of the *Evening Post*, New York:

Ever since the controversy began, some two months since, concerning the correctness with which Mr. Frothingham has narrated the incidents of John Brown's connection with Gerrit Smith, appeals have been made to me as one who ought to take some part in the dispute. To all such I have answered that nothing but absolute necessity,—by which I meant an exigency I could not properly decline to meet,—would draw me into a controversy so painful. I had privately answered the questions of those who had a right to seek information; and I had publicly stated (in the *Atlantic Monthly* for 1875) what I thought the public had a right to know. But now that exigency seems to have arisen, and I therefore desire to say, in your columns, that my own first knowledge of the plans of John Brown for invading the South and forcibly emancipating slaves,—the same plans he afterwards attempted to execute in Virginia,—was obtained from Brown in Gerrit Smith's house at Peterboro, N. Y., February 22, 1858, and in the presence of

Mr. Smith himself, with whom I discussed them fully on that day, the following day, and again on the 24th of May, 1858, at the Revere House in Boston.

I do not mean that every detail of those plans was then, or afterward, talked over between Mr. Smith and myself; but I do mean that we talked, or heard John Brown talk, on the subject for at least six hours, and probably for more than ten hours; until the general features of his enterprise became as well known to me, and, as I have always supposed, to Mr. Smith, as are the general scope and methods of most undertakings in which men deliberately engage. We two, Mr. Smith, then sixty-one years old, and myself, a little turned of twenty-six, on the 23d of February, 1858, at about the hour of sunset, did deliberately and earnestly engage with each other that we would stand by and support John Brown in his undertaking, for reasons which Mr. Frothingham set forth in our very words, so far as I can remember them. Up to the day of John Brown's capture at Harper's Ferry, in October, 1859, that engagement was faithfully kept. Whatever we had encouraged Brown to expect of us in that matter, so far as it seemed possible, we two, the old Abolitionist and the young Republican, punctually and exactly did, each in his own way. And I have yet to learn that John Brown, up to the day of his death, ever doubted that we had done so, or that we would have done more if we could. Neither of us, probably, was ever fully and coolly convinced of the wisdom of his scheme. Mr. Smith wrote me, May 7, 1858 (a letter still in existence), that he never was so convinced; yet he aided it then, as he had done before, and as he did afterwards. I corresponded with him frequently about it, for a year and a half,—that is, from March, 1858, to September, 1859, in which month I believe I sent to Mr. Smith the last of many letters I received from Brown. First and last, I probably sent Mr. Smith twenty letters of Brown's, and received from him perhaps as many which related to this affair. These letters I destroyed in 1859-60, or so many of them as were then in my hands; but some that were then in possession of other persons,—Theodore Parker, Wentworth Higginson, or Dr. Howe,—escaped destruction, and are now in existence.

At no time during the nineteen months between February 19, 1858 (when, as I suppose, Gerrit Smith first heard of Brown's plan from Brown himself, and in Smith's Peterboro house), and October 18, 1859, when we heard of Brown's capture, did Mr. Smith intimate to me that he had ceased to support and aid the plan; nor, in fact, did he cease to aid it. When he wrote me that " as things now stand it seems to me it would be madness to attempt to execute it " (May 7, 1858), he had just given money to aid it; and within a month afterward he gave money again. He allowed Brown to take the responsibility of failure,—only warning him that, *at that time*, it would be " a certain and most disastrous failure." Such was then my own opinion, and when Smith met, at his own room in the Revere House, Boston, May 24, 1858, with Theodore Parker, Dr. Howe, George L. Stearns, and myself, to decide whether Brown should be allowed to go on at that time, Mr. Smith was an active participant in the discussion. It resulted in sending Brown back to Kansas until such a time as he could more safely undertake his Southern campaign.

My recollection is clear that Mr. Smith then fully understood the matter, and unreservedly sanctioned the agreement, as Brown himself stated it to Colonel Higginson, and as I remember it,—viz., that Brown should go to Kansas for the summer and autumn of 1858, but

should be aided to begin his Southern campaign in the
winter and spring of 1859, when two or three thousand
dollars should be raised for him by Messrs. Stearns,
Smith, and the rest of us.   In accordance with this agreement, in the following spring (April, 1859) Brown presented himself at Peterboro, after delivering his twelve
forcibly emancipated Missouri slaves in Canada, and received from Mr. Smith there a subscription of four hundred dollars, part of which was a note of E. B. Whitman,
of Kansas, payable to Smith, and which Brown considered
the same as money.   With some of this four hundred
dollars, or with money afterwards sent by Mr. Smith,
Brown paid, in part, for his pikes, at Collinsville, Connecticut, to arm the slaves of Virginia.   I presume Mr.
Smith never knew that his gift would be so used; but he
put no restrictions on its use, and he knew that Brown
was then on his slow way to execute the plan unfolded
to us at Peterboro the winter before.   Again, when, in
August, 1859, Brown wrote me from Chambersburg, that
he still wanted three hundred dollars with which to begin the attack, I sent his letter to Smith, who at once
sent Brown a draft for a hundred dollars on the State
Bank of Albany.   I suppose this was his last contribution
to Brown, and I am certain it was sent with a full *general*
knowledge of what Brown would do with it.

How then could Mr. Smith, G. L. Stearns, and Dr.
Howe deny, as they all did, that they knew nothing of
the Harper's Ferry attack?   Simply because they did
not know, or perhaps guess, that Brown meant to begin
there.   We expected he would go farther west, into a region less accessible, where his movements might escape
notice for weeks, except as the alleged acts of some ma-
rauding party.   In this respect, and in this alone, so far
as I know, he changed his plans of 1858, which had been

fully explained to Smith, Howe, and Stearns. Being called
to testify at Washington, the two last named (as they
both told me) found the questions of the Senate Committee so unskillfully framed that they could, without
literal falsehood, answer as they did. I do not say they
were justified in this, but such was their own opinion.
Probably Gerrit Smith felt also justified, at the time,
in making public statements which told a part of the
truth, but not the whole. He was not a witness at Washington, being an asylum patient at Utica in that agitated
winter of 1859-60; but in 1860 and again in 1867 he
published papers which, had I seen them in manuscript,
as I did that of 1874, I should have protested against
their publication, as I did with the more exact statement
of the latter year. I only saw them after publication,
too late to protest. But from 1867 until his death in
December, 1874, I was resolved to persuade my old
friend, if possible, to publish something more in keeping
with the facts, and with his own magnanimity. I therefore took some pains to preserve my own recollections
and those of two other persons, who, like myself, had
known Brown's plans, and Smith's connection with them,
and in the *Atlantic Monthly*, for July, 1872, printed the
narrative thus obtained, with many omissions of name
and circumstance, in deference to what seemed Mr. Smith's
sensitiveness. At some interval after this, but not until
I had been urged by many, both friends and strangers,
to tell the story of Brown more fully, I sent this letter
to Mr. Smith, with whom I had kept up an occasional
correspondence since 1859:

"Concord, Mass., Oct. 13, 1872.

"My dear Sir:

"I have often been urged to publish what I knew of
John Brown and his plans, more especially of late, since

the appearance of some papers, respecting him in the
Atlantic Monthly. I am inclined to think the proper
time has come for me to do so: but as I was first acquainted with those plans in your house at Peterboro,
where I spent a day or two with Brown in the winter of
1857-58, I do not feel at liberty to make such publication without consulting you. May I ask if there is any
reason, in your opinion, why the whole truth should not
now be told, without respect of persons? We were witnesses, and in some sense participants, in a great historical event, in regard to which the evidence (on which
the truth of history must rest) is every year passing
away, by the death of persons and the decay of recollections. I met, a week or two since, the last survivor,
among Brown's men, of the tragic fight at Harper's
Ferry,—Osborne Anderson, who seems to be declining
in consumption. Before all the witnesses are dead, would
it not be wise to put upon record the authentic facts, in
time to have any errors in the statement pointed out and
corrected?

" Yours very truly,

" F. B. Sanborn."

To this Mr. Smith replied on the 19th, and Mrs.
Smith on the 20th of October, thus:

" F. B. Sanborn, Esq.,

" Dear Friend: I have your esteemed letter. I am
not competent to advise in the case. When the Harper's
Ferry affair occurred I was sick, and my brain somewhat
diseased. That affair excited and shocked me, and a
few weeks after I was taken to a Lunatic Asylum. From
that day to this I have had but a hazy view of dear John

Brown's great work. Indeed, some of my impressions of it have, as others have told me, been quite erroneous and even wild. I would not, therefore, presume to pass any judgment in the case. Let me, however, say that my brain has continued to the present time to be sensitive in this John Brown matter, and that every now and then I get little or no sleep in consequence. It was so when I read the articles in the *Atlantic* you refer to. And now your bare proposition to write of this matter has given me another sleepless turn. In every such turn I fear a recurrence of my insanity.

" I must not ask you to make so much account of my health. Nevertheless, if you could defer your contemplated work until after my death (not long hence, as I am approaching seventy-six) you would lay me under great obligations to your kindness. So, too, you would, if in case you write it before my death [you should] make as sparing a use of my name as possible.

" Poor Osborne Anderson! I was personally acquainted with him. I lament his declining health. Give the brave and noble man my love, and the enclosed ten dollars. Mrs. Smith and I would be happy to see you and yours at our home.

" Cordially yours,

" GERRIT SMITH."

" Peterboro, Oct. 20, 1872.
" My dear Mr. Sanborn:

" Everything concerning dear John Brown is, in Mr. Smith's mind, so closely linked with his insanity, that the bare reading of your esteemed letter brought that painful passage of his life back again most vividly, causing a rush of blood to his head, and an almost sleepless night. I greatly fear the effect on him of any further written history of John Brown. Yet, if you deem it necessary for the public good, and see it to be clearly your duty to write that history *now*, I have no right to say a word against it. Only let me ask you, if you should write, to use Mr. Smith's name as little as possible.

"Give my love to Mrs. Sanborn. We would be very happy, at any time, to receive a visit from you both.

"Sincerely your friend,
"ANN C. SMITH."

This pathetic response, unlike any that I had expected, affected me deeply, and showed me, to my sorrow, that I had too long delayed to ask the important question. I reflected much on this new aspect of things, consulted my friends, Edwin Morton, Dr. Howe, and Wendell Phillips, who differed in opinion as to what my duty was, and finally replied thus:

"Concord, Nov. 18, 1872.
"My dear Sir:

"I have delayed answering your note of the 19th October, containing a proposition on the subject of my proposed reminiscences of John Brown, because I did not wish to answer without due consideration. I am not satisfied that the course you suggest is the wisest or best; but such is my regard for your wishes in the matter (as testified by my silence heretofore) that I am willing to accede to it as far as concerns all mention of yourself. I doubt whether I have the right any longer to withhold information on other points, where the truth is liable to be obscured or misrepresented in course of years: and therefore I cannot pledge myself farther. And I could wish that all of us who had cognizance, in a greater or less degree, of John Brown's plans, would commit to paper their recollection of the facts, for mutual examination and correction: publication may be deferred till all are convinced that the proper time has come. I urge this upon all whom I see or correspond with; having no other wish in the matter than that the whole and exact truth shall be eventually known to the world, as it is now known to God and John Brown.

"I regret that my former communication should have caused you any uneasiness, though I cannot reproach myself in the matter, since I only took the friendly and direct course in addressing you on the subject. Pray present my regards to Mrs. Smith, by whose note I was deeply touched, and believe me ever

"Yours very truly,

"F. B. SANBORN."

To this letter Mr. Smith responded in a few days, and in these words:

"Nov. 24, 1872.

"My dear Friend:

"I have your letter. Your tender regard for my peace of mind touches my heart and calls out gratitude. I thank you warmly for concluding to omit the mention of my name in what you write. I wish that when you have written it, you would visit me (at my expense) and read it to me. You can help me to clear up my cloudy recollections, and then I may see nothing in the way of your adding my name to other names in your narrative. My wife joins me in love to yourself and wife. Bring her with you when you visit us.

"Cordially yours,

"GERRIT SMITH."

I did not, of course, accept this invitation on the terms mentioned, but in one of my journeys with my son Thomas, in July, 1874, I took Peterboro in my way home, and there spent two pleasant days, talking with the Smiths concerning the plans and achievements of Brown, about which I was beginning to write the papers that came out in the *Atlantic* for 1875. I found no serious want of harmony in our recollections, except that mine were more distinct, and that they both were strongly impressed that Brown contemplated the escape of slaves to Canada. That was indeed one alternative, to be adopted if he could not maintain himself on slave territory, as he hoped. This phase of the question will appear in the paper soon to be cited. It had been :n my hands six months when I visited Peterboro for the last time. Late in 1873, upon some occasion now forgotten, I had written to Mrs. Smith gently renewing my request for a statement from Mr. Smith. I kept no copy, but the tenor of my note may be inferred from my answer from Mrs. Smith, who wrote me thus:

                " Peterboro, Jan. 1, 1874.

" Dear Mr. Sanborn:

" I have received and read your good letter, but I cannot yet read it to Mr. Smith. The painful sensations continue in his brain, and his physician wishes him to be kept from all excitement, as there is a tendency to congestion. His memory is so confused concerning the things connected with his insanity, that I think it would be impossible for him to make a correct statement. As soon as I find it will do to bring the matter before him, I will do so, and let you know the result.

" Affectionately,

" Ann C. Smith."

Soon after this came the following paper by Mr. Smith, to which his wife added a postscript, Mr. Smith an amendatory note, and I an indorsement. This sheet I hold, and it was among the papers given by me to Mr. Frothingham for perusal. No part of it has ever before been printed:

" *Copy of a Statement signed by Gerrit Smith, January 3,* *1874, but Drawn up in the Handwriting of Mrs. Smith,* *who has added a Postscript, to which her own signature* *is attached.*

" Agreeably to the suggestion in Mr. Sanborn's letter to Mrs. Smith, I give an account of my acquaintance with some of John Brown's movements. I dictate the writing, and make it very brief, because I am suffering from an attack of vertigo.

" Mr. Edwin Morton, of Boston, was for several years a member of my family. During that time Mr. Frank B. Sanborn, of Concord, Massachusetts, repeatedly visited him. They were classmates in Harvard University. On his visit in February, 1858, he met John Brown, who often took my home in his way between Kansas and his residence in Essex County, New York. He and Mr. Sanborn were much in Mr. Morton's room. I was in it a part or all of the time whilst Brown was reading his plan for entering the South and summoning the slaves to the mountains, where they could defend themselves and thence escape to Canada. This plan, I have been informed, was drawn up by himself not long before, under the roof of Mr. Frederick Douglass in Rochester. My heart responded to his merciful interest in the victims of oppression, and he had my warmest wishes for his success. I had but little conversation with Brown respecting his enterprise. He told me he was not yet decided in what State to begin it. As the execution of it was long delayed, I thought it was abandoned. His invasion of Harper's Ferry in the fall of 1859 grew, as I supposed, out of an entirely new and suddenly adopted plan. I was astonished to hear of it, so unlike was it to that of going to the mountains. I came afterwards to believe that this invasion was in pursuance of the revival of his old plan.

" He addressed a large anti-slavery meeting in this village in April, 1859. I never saw him after that time, and I kept up no communication with him. Hearing, some months after through another person, that he was in Chambersburg and in need of money, I directed a hundred dollars to be sent to him. His being there led me to believe that he was on his way to the mountains of Maryland or Virginia.

" Brown was a brave and noble and emphatically religious man. He lived for his race, and especially for the wronged and unfortunate. I had frequent dealings with him. From first to last he purchased three farms from me. He was the patron and friend of my little colored colony in his neighborhood. I frequently gave him moneys to promote his slave-delivering and other benevolent purposes,—in the aggregate, however, only about a thousand dollars. This would have been none too much to compensate him for his self-sacrificing interest in my colony. His dependence for means to execute his Southern undertaking was, as he informed me, mainly on the good and generous Mr. Stearns, of Boston.

" It is but proper for me to say that I have dictated

this writing with some distrust of my recollections, both because the occurrences were so many years ago, and because of my severe illness in the latter part of 1859 and the early part of 1860.

(Signed)   "GERRIT SMITH.

" Peterboro, Jan. 3, 1874."

" Mr. Sanborn will do what he pleases with the foregoing statement, provided he shall have Mr. Morton's consent. Mr. Smith would not have the name of any living person used in this connection without such person's consent. Immediately after the Harper's Ferry affair he destroyed all the letters touching Brown's movements which he had received from persons in any degree privy to those movements; and he took it for granted that his own similar letters to others had also been destroyed.

(Signed)   "ANN C. SMITH."

Mr. Smith afterwards (January 18th), through Mr. Morton, whom I saw every day or two at his law office in Boston, requested me to " strike out the sentence beginning ' I never saw him after that time,' and supply its place with the following sentence,—' I never saw him after that time, and I had no further communication with him save a single exchange of letters regarding a note for $250 which I held against him.' "

Upon the original sheet containing the above statements, after showing them to Edwin Morton, I endorsed these words: " According to the distinct recollections of Mr. Morton and myself, the above statement is incomplete, and fails to give the more important facts of the case. We can therefore make no public use of it.

(Signed)   "F. B. SANBORN.

" Concord, Jan. 25, 1874."

In my reply to Mrs. Smith a week earlier (January 16, 1874) I had explained to her that all the compromising letters in my possession at the time of the arrest of Brown, and all that came to me in the following winter, from the archives of the Brown family at North Elba, were destroyed by me; but some held by others escaped. I was, in fact, visited by Colonel Charles Miller, Mr. Smith's son-in-law, in October, 1859, to make sure, on Mr. Smith's account, that his letters were destroyed,— he having previously visited John Brown, Jr., in Ohio, for the same purpose, as he told me.

Brief and incomplete as Mr. Smith's latest statement was, it has yet much importance as a piece of evidence. It supplies some omissions in his printed declaration of 1867, and directly contradicts an earlier declaration (of 1860) in a vital point. But it omits to say that Brown had been in Smith's house four days when I arrived; that Brown had expressly named that house as a place of secret meeting for Parker, Stearns, Higginson, and myself; that my sole errand there was to meet Brown and his friends, while Brown's sole errand was to lay before us in secret his long-cherished scheme. Mrs. Smith's postscript supplies one important fact,—that Mr. Smith himself directed the destruction of papers relating to Brown, and supposed that others had taken the same precaution, as I certainly had. The inference from all these documents is so plain that I need not stop to point it out.

Indeed, I have written thus far with sorrow and reluctance,—feelings constantly mine ever since the public attitude taken by Mr. Smith in the year 1860. To me he assumed no such attitude, but was ever ready to declare that my memory of the affair was better than his, and at my last interviews, in July, 1874, five months

preceding his death, he said the same. I have no re-
proaches to bring against him.

He was my friend, faithful and just to me;

yet I could not fail to see that from some cause to me
unknown, alienation of mind, regard for those whom he
loved, or perhaps the moral perplexity that so often
besets such a crisis as that in which John Brown and his
friends found themselves in 1859-60, Gerrit Smith had
swerved from what Wordsworth, in his " Dion " calls the

Ideal path of right,
More fair than Heaven's broad causeway paved with stars.

I have never been able to satisfy myself, and cannot,
therefore, hope to explain to others the reason why Mr.
Smith shrank from a full disclosure, and preferred to
pass away with the secret unspoken. It was not for lack
of courage or of magnanimity, certainly not for lack of
admiration of Brown and his deed; nor through any
disloyalty to those, living or dead, associated with Gerrit Smith in that and other enterprises undertaken for
liberty. Nor was it, I venture to say, with any futile
hope of averting the course of history, or mitigating the
verdict of mankind. Gerrit Smith was not of that quality
or temper of soul; he was, like Dion,

Of spirit too capacious to require
That Destiny her course should change; too just
To his own native greatness to desire
That wretched boon, days lengthened by mistrust.

I prefer to retain that opinion which I early formed of

my venerable friend; his errors of judgment were but
the slight accidents of human frailty, not to be cited as
instances of a character that, in all essential traits, was
lofty, generous, and self-devoted.

F. B. SANBORN.

CONCORD, March 15, 1878.

The exigency contemplated when I wrote as
above, soon passed away. General Cochrane
visited me in Concord, saw the letters of his uncle
and aunt, and was satisfied that I had told the
truth. He withdrew his misapprehensions, and
sent me, as evidence of confidence, the fine portraits of the Smiths which have since ornamented
my hall, with those of Emerson, Thoreau, and
Walt Whitman, the latter, in his broad and loving
humanity, and a little in his personality, recalling
Gerrit Smith. I have since printed biographies
of Brown and Dr. Howe, in which the story of the
Harper's Ferry foray, so far as Brown's secret
committee was involved, has been told; the son of
Major Stearns has published a life of his father, and
the daughter of Dr. Howe has done the same. In
these books other facts appear. I print this old
letter, that the record may be complete, and less
room be left for vexatious disputes after Colonel
Higginson and myself are gone.

During this eventful winter of 1859-60, our as-
sociate in the conspiracy of Brown, Theodore
Parker, was in Rome, vainly seeking to postpone
the hour of his own death, by foreign residence.
He died in Florence in the following May and is

buried there, under a monument designed by the hand of his friend, the sculptor Story. Before Parker knew accurately the facts concerning Gerret Smith, and while he was anticipating that Dr. Howe, and perhaps myself, might join him in Italy, he wrote as follows to Smith, whom he knew well. The copy came to me in Mrs. Parker's clear handwriting, along with the mass of manuscripts she bequeathed to me at her own death in 1875.

"ROME, 16th Feb., 1860.

My dear Mr. Smith:

It is with great pain that I have heard of the illness which the recent distressing events have brought on your much-enduring frame, which was so shattered by illness before. When I saw you last I did not think that my next letter would be from such a place or for such a purpose. But such is the uncertainty of all mortal things. Some of the rumors relate that you will perhaps come to Europe for health. If this be so, I trust I shall have the good fortune to meet you somewhere. We have many Americans at Rome,—two or three hundred, it is said,— of whom about forty are from Boston, not to mention the permanent inhabitants. So you see one need not lack companionship. Besides, here are many more from Massachusetts and New England.

I feel great anxiety about the immediate future of America; the remote future I have no doubts about. We must see much darker hours before it is daylight, —darker and also bloody, I think ; for nations seldom settle their difficulties without *passion*—& so without what comes of passion. The Slaveholders are in great wrath. I am waiting for the Supreme Court of the United States, (in the Lemmon case), to decide, as it must, that a master *may* take his slaves in transit through a free State, &

keep them in it a reasonable time, subject not only to his own caprice, but defiant of the Laws of that State. Certainly, the Slaveholders *must* have *eminent domain* over the free States & bondage *must* exercise *Right of way* in New York & New England.—Next year, or the year after, it *must* decide for the African Slave trade! " There is one *general grievance*," said Oliver Cromwell in the House of Commons, " & that is the LAW ! "

But I did not mean to worry you with a long letter, so with heartiest sympathy for your sufferings and profound respect for your Character & services, believe me,

Faithfully and truly yours,

THEODORE PARKER.

When I wrote my first biography of John Brown, for the History of his native Connecticut township, Torrington, I told the story of Mr. Smith's connection with the Virginia plans, in substance as I have told it here. But I inserted in the small edition separately printed, a few copies of a fac-simile of a note from Brown to his son, John Brown, Jr., which has never elsewhere been published, I believe. I put some twenty copies of this volume, with the heliotyped sheet bound in,— the unmistakable script of Brown—in a few libraries, for reference, in case anyone should have doubts about its authenticity. It is found on page 144.

Up to this time I had not supposed that John Brown was present at the Pottawatomie executions in May,—relying too much on the statements of Redpath and the brother of Brown, without asking from Brown himself the exact truth in the matter. I had, therefore, stated my belief too positively in my book of 1878. But late in 1879 (December 6), James Townsley, one of Brown's company on that occasion, made a full statement confessing his own presence and participation, and charging that Brown had fired one of the fatal shots that night. This was not true; but in the main I have found out that Townsley was truthful. Soon after this matter was brought to my knowledge, I sought an interview with Owen Brown, who was also present at the deed, and obtained from him the precise account which I published in my second "Life of Brown," in 1885 (pages 267-70). I then learned that most of Brown's family who were not with him that night were as ignorant as I had been of what Brown had done, although he had always admitted his responsibility for the deed. There were many in Kansas, however, who had reason to know that John Brown was present and commanding in that tragedy; and when I visited Kansas for the first time in 1882, I saw several men who had long known, or been morally certain of the facts. I have seen no reason to doubt that this execution was one of the sad necessities of the times, fully justified in Brown's mind and that of the most of the residents in Kansas. But it was made the occasion for much vilification of Brown and his friends by the men whom the fame of Brown had eclipsed, or who had honestly differed from him in their judgment of what the need of the time

was. The opinions of good men will always dif-
fer, I suppose, as to the merit or demerit of Brown
in ordering these executions, and seeing them performed. It is the belief of the best authorities
in Kansas history that the men slain had a suffi-
cent, though irregular trial. That they had well
earned their violent death, under their own code of
violence, is now quite clear; the pretense of their
innocence is a sham, invented by men who knew
better, and accepted by ignorant or half-informed
persons, who would justify the killing of a bur-
glar, but shudder at the wild justice of lynch law,
—sometimes the best code for semi-barbarous com-
munities. I have in my book cited the testimony
and opinions of the Free State men of Kansas; but
here is a bit of evidence that will be new to most of
my readers. General Shelby, a Missourian, who
joined his pro-slavery neighbors in trying to force
slavery upon Kansas, and who rose to be a briga-
dier in the Confederate service, was afterward " re-
constructed " and made United States marshal of
western Missouri. To a friend of mine, who knew
him well while holding that office, and residing at
Kansas City in Missouri, he said in substance:

" Brown was right, and did just what he ought to have
done in killing the Doyles and others at Pottawatomie.
I would have done in Missouri what he did in Kansas.
I was myself in Kansas fighting the Free-State men—
had no business there on any such errand, and ought to
have been shot for being there. John Brown was the only
man then in Kansas who seemed to realize fully the

situation. He would have shot me, perhaps, if he had met me in Kansas,—and it would have been no more than his duty."

Among other Kansas authorities I cited August Bondi, a German Jew, who early settled in Kansas and served under John Brown in May and June, 1856. He afterward became the police magistrate of Salina, a considerable town in Kansas, and died there at a good old age a year or two since. His daughter called at my residence in Concord the past summer. I quoted freely in my "Life and Letters of John Brown" from the German and English publications of Judge Bondi, and from his letters to me; but at his request I abstained from publishing a letter of his, written early in 1884, long before my book was published. There is now no reason why it should be withheld from publication, since both he and his friend, Theodore Wiener (commonly called "Weiner") are dead. Wiener took part in the Pottawatomie executions of May 24, 1856, but Bondi did not. Dating at Salina, January 25, 1884, he wrote me:

" At the instance of many friends I concluded to publish my [German] articles on John Brown in English also; and in the Salina *Herald* of yesterday I commenced. . . . You say in your last that I relate some things that no one else does, which is just what hundreds have told me before. Still, I have carefully refrained from stating anything I could not implicitly vouch for. Newspaper correspondents of those days would not, *dared* not, give him the credit he deserved; because if they had, Robinson, Jim Lane, Pomeroy, etc., would have dwindled into insignificance. And John Brown, while he cared about results, never was very anxious to have them credited to himself. There always were, even in 1856, secret intrigues at work to detract from his achievements; so we need not be astonished if living dogs continue to bark at the dead lion. John Brown was the most affectionate of parents, the kindest of friends, and at every opportunity he lectured, instructed and admonished us boys, just as I report. For nothing did I admire him so much as for the conversion of my friend Wiener from a rank pro-slavery man to an uncompromising abolitionist.

" Theodore Wiener is a Jew, as I am, and as Benjamin was. He came from Germany in 1847, and merchandized in the southern States, coming to St. Louis in 1854. There Benjamin and myself became acquainted with him. We two left St. Louis for Kansas early in 1855; as we parted from Wiener, he wished that the Southerners would assist us to an early return. [As being anti-slavery men, not wanted in Kansas.] In September, 1855, Benjamin returned to St. Louis, when Wiener consented to come to Kansas and open a store on my claim at Musquito Creek, four miles from Dutch Henry's Crossing, pledging himself to Benjamin that he would run his store and let politics alone. Wiener then invested from seven to eight thousand dollars in goods and went to Kansas—I, in the meantime, being very sick, had left for St. Louis two days before he reached my claim. So I did not see Wiener again till about May, 1856, when he came to St. Louis to buy goods, and I returned to Kansas with him. Judge of my surprise when he conversed with me as a radical Free State man; and he was free to acknowledge that the change was mainly due to his intimacy with the Browns.

" When the Pottawatomie and Osawatomie Rifles, in which companies the Browns were, started May 21, 1856, to assist Lawrence, some 65 men in all, Wiener furnished them as a gift all the necessary provisions. His store was soon after completely plundered; and I think no Free State man lost as much in actual money that year as Wiener did. His loss footed up some $8,000; some of the men in Lawrence presented bills for greater losses, but of course there was no such actual loss.

" It might be said that Brown's sons followed him to the fight of Black Jack prompted by filial affection, (as they were); Kaiser and myself, who were fresh from the battlefields of Europe, did likewise from our sympathy for Liberty. Cochrane and the Moores had been outraged by the Border Ruffians in their own persons and families. But what else caused the presence of the merchant Wiener in that camp, but the spiritual power wielded by that hero of truth and virtue, who conquered the friend of slavery by the attraction of a superior mind? I always considered the proselyting of Wiener a greater feat than the victory at Black Jack.

" Wiener, who took part in the so-called Pottawatomie massacre, has never to any extent conversed with me about it; he never would allow himself to be drawn out. I have a theory of my own on that matter,—a suspicion that Wilkinson was a Mason, as Wiener is, and that Wiener at the time did not know that fact. Should I, during my travels in next Fall's political campaign, happen in Wiener's neighborhood, I will see him and try to persuade him to tell what he knows."

At the date of this letter James Townsley had

made his confession of participation in the executions at Dutch Henry's, but I think Wiener
never made any statement public concerning it.
A year later than this (January, 1885), but before
the publication of my book, my friend, Dr. H. L.
Wayland, then of Philadelphia, sent me a letter of
Frederick Douglass, afterwards printed in the
" National Baptist " of February 12, 1885, which
is worth preserving:

" I have never been able to entirely explain and recon-
cile the heroic conduct of Captain Brown with that gen-
tleness of temper and tenderness of heart which he always
exhibited among his friends, and especially in the presence of little children.   He spent a number of weeks in
my house at Rochester,* and I had many opportunities
to get a peep into his soul; and in it I found the highest
sense of justice, a sincere love of mankind, and a total
absence of selfishness.   There was another thing about
him quite remarkable.   No matter how inconsistent, impossible and desperate a thing might appear to others,
if John Brown said he would do it, he was sure to be
believed.   His words were never taken for empty bravado.
.   .   .   We are still too near his times to judge him
broadly and justly."

An old townsman of Brown's at Hudson, in
Ohio (Mr. Loren Case, who died a few years ago),
left this interesting reminiscence of his friend:—

" The last time I saw John Brown was in Hudson,
(1859) a short time before he went to Harper's Ferry.
The night before, he had spoken in Ellsworth Hall, on
* In January and February, 1858.

the corner opposite the Catholic church. His topic was the Declaration of Independence; his main effort was to show what it cost the old pioneers of Liberty to gain and maintain their rights for themselves and their posterity; many of whom, having pledged their lives, fortunes and sacred honor to maintain these liberties, sealed the pledge with their blood. I met him on his way to the train the next morning. He was walking with his hands behind him, in deep thought, seemingly not noticing me until I got within reach of his hand, which then came quickly from the skirt of his coat to grasp mine, and the greeting came with his cheerful voice and smile. The topic of the night before was still on his mind. He said he could not do justice to it when he spoke; could not find words to express himself, nor impress the minds of his hearers, especially those who profess to be one with Him who came to break the yoke and let the oppressed go free. Such Christians were guilty of that sin of the Pharisees, hypocrisy, denounced by Christ; and if they did not break the American yoke and let the slaves go free, they would have to suffer the penalty, pronounced against the Pharisees, even if it took away their lives and their fortunes."

This was the constant warning given by Brown, which the Civil War verified. The last letter which he sent to Ohio from his Charlestown prison was to this same Mr. Case; in it he said—(December 2, 1859, the very morning of his death):

" Your most kind and cheering letter of Nov. 25 is received. Such an outburst of warm-hearted sympathy, not only for myself, but also for those who have no helper, compels me to steal a moment from those allowed me in which to prepare for my last great change, in order to send you a few words. Such a feeling as you manifest makes you to shine (in my estimation) in the midst of a wicked and perverse generation, as a light in the world. May you ever prove yourself equal to the high estimate I have placed on you! Pure and undefiled religion before God and the Father is, as I understand it, an active, (not a dormant) principle.

" I do not undertake to direct any more about my children. I leave that now entirely to their excellent mother, from whom I have just parted. I send you my ' salutation with my own hand.' Remember me to all yours and my dear friends.

" Your friend,

" JOHN BROWN."

Mr. Case, to whom this characteristic letter was sent, was six years younger than Brown, and had been his Sunday-school pupil in Hudson, before 1820. Of Brown's manner of speaking in youth, Mr. Case said:

" He had a very mild way to express his views, especially to the young, and in a practical manner to show the true principle of Christianity, that it was more to give than to receive. In conversation, or when debating with others, if they showed anger in their expression or gestures, he would stand with his hands folded behind him, and in a very calm, decided way utter his views, without raising his hand to give force to his argument; but he showed by the motion of his head and body that it came from the heart to convince you."

In the years when I knew Brown, this calmness of manner sometimes gave way to animated speech and gestures,—so deeply did he feel the coldness of those he addressed on his one great subject; but on his trial, the mildness of his earlier manner returned to him, and his last speech was delivered with all the quiet and moderation which Mr. Case describes. This mild and humble Christian, this practical disciple of Jefferson, was a pioneer and hero of emancipation. Others had much share in that work,—but its two chief martyrs were John Brown and Abraham Lincoln,— of whom one began and the other completed the forcible freeing of 4,000,000 slaves in the United States. In oratory, too, their names will stand connected; for Emerson declared that Brown's speech after conviction and Lincoln's Gettysburg oration were the high-water mark of eloquence in the nineteenth century.